So Very Much the Best of Us

Dec. 2017

Dear Seab,

Now that I work for the Church I always feel like I have to have a disclaimer of sorts when I give as even REMOTELY religious gift, ha. Some of these stories are pretty Catholic, but they're all very uplifting, and it's a book that's given me comfort in tough times. They're also brief, because I can't imagine you've got a ton of time to read with Fynn and Lylah running around all day. Hope you like it! Merry Christmas! Love you so much!

♡ Rebecca

So Very Much the Best of Us

*Prayers of Praise
in Prose*

BRIAN DOYLE

SO VERY MUCH THE BEST OF US
Prayers of Praise in Prose

by Brian Doyle

Edited by Gregory F. Augustine Pierce
Cover design by Ian Courter
Cover photo, "Mandrill," by James Balog, jamesbalog.com
Interior drawings by Mary Miller Doyle
Text design and typesetting by Patricia A. Lynch

Copyright © 2015 by Brian Doyle

Published by ACTA Publications, 4848 N. Clark Street, Chicago, IL 60640, (800) 397-2282, www.actapublications.com

Library of Congress Catalog number: 2015948509
ISBN: 978-0-87946-549-0
Printed in the United States of America by Total Printing Systems
Year 25 24 23 22 21 20 19 18 17 16 15
Printing 15 14 13 12 11 10 9 8 7 6 5 4 3 2 First

♻ Text printed on 30% post-consumer recycled paper

for my friend John McPhee,
with thanks for countless hours
of exuberant grinning story-trading

CONTENTS

XI.

XII.

THE PROMISE
OF AMERICAN CATHOLICISM

Look, is the Holy Roman Catholic Church in America, and surely abroad, a flawed often-greedy often-idiotic sometimes-corrupt corporation complete with fools and mountebanks and criminals and prim souls afraid of change and niggling for power?

Sure it is.

But that's the crust, the surface, a part of the package, not at all the whole package; and those who sneer at Catholicism, and tar all with the brush that should paint a few, are fools. For Catholicism in America, and surely abroad, is and always has been a wilder adventure than we admit. It's about men and women and children and how they live their lives trying to find the light and mercy behind all things. It's about people muddling along trying to find and share love. It's not about rules and regulations. It's not about Not. On the much deeper level it is not about what should be prevented but about what is possible. On the deepest level it is so revolutionary that we hardly ever whisper or acknowledge or roar that truth. But it's so.

At its essence Catholicism says that all beings are holy and Christ is a splinter in every single heart, even the twisted and brooding ones, and our job is not to wag fingers and pronounce judgment but to reach for the broken and the hopeless and the starving and the naked and the jailed and do whatever we can to witness and heal and celebrate them, for they are Christ, every bit the Christ that a pope is.

If you are like me you are delighted by Pope Francis, whose first words as *Il Papa* were *I am a sinner*. Now there's a guy with some refreshing humility, who gets it that a small tight cadre of rigid believers is so very sensible in a world so rife with chance and chaos, but that such a cadre will only change the world by demonstrating true humility while finding new ways through the walls that people erect around themselves.

I have no patience with those walls anymore. This book is an attempt to find new ways through and around walls. I want to poke around mercy and love and tenderness and laughter and engagement with others. I think those are the weapons that will destroy greed and violence. I think those are the deep weapons of Catholicism. I think that's what Catholicism in my beloved bedraggled brave country is, at its best.

Maybe you do, too, in which case thank you for being my team-mate.

Brian Doyle
Portland, Oregon

I.

CONFIRMATION DAY

The day I was granted the Sacrament of Confirmation and was admitted with full rights and privileges to the Church Eternal got off to a slow start, because the bishop was late; there had been a rain delay at the Mets game, but His Excellency couldn't just *leave* the stadium, because the Mets were playing the Pirates, and this was the Pirates team with Roberto Clemente and Willie Stargell and Dock Ellis (who would pitch a no-hitter a month later while stoned out of his mind), and anyway the Mets were coming off their shocking championship the year before, so who would leave on account of a little downpour?

We waited in the school auditorium as our parents and grandparents and disgruntled brothers and sisters rustled in the searing heat of the church. It was a roaring hot day and someone in the choir fainted. My dad said later he could hear a hole exactly the size of an alto in the choir's subsequent performance, but we think he was teasing us. Finally the bishop arrived, having left in a huff when the Mets made their fourth error of the day, and the ceremony started.

Our older brothers and sisters, who had already been Confirmed and were pretty smug about it and claimed there were secret rituals and code words they could never reveal to us on pain of death, had filled us with stories of the bishop slapping kids in the face as part of the ancient Sacrament, and while none of us could figure out why exactly a slap figured in a ceremony that seemed to be about welcoming new members to the army, we were suitably forewarned, and there was a lot of loose talk about slapping the bishop back, and ducking his hand, and bobbing and weaving like Muhammad Ali, or catching his hand as it came hurtling toward your face and leaning in companionably and whispering *not this time, big fella,* and remarks like that, mostly from the boys, although two of the girls, I remember, were coldly intent on slapping anyone who slapped them, and one girl said she would accept the first blow and turn her other cheek for a second slap, but we thought she was just trying to impress Sister Marie.

The Mets lost the game finally 7 to 4, and just as we started up the aisle, two by two, boys to the west and girls to the east, a flurry of fathers and older brothers arrived in the back of the church and the heat rose noticeably. The choir started into Onward Christian Soldiers and someone, we think our dad, said the words *breakaway Anglican cult* loud enough for the whole back of the church to ripple. I looked at my older brother as I went past our family's pew and he made a gesture like a bishop slapping a kid so hard the kid's spectacles flew off and my heart quailed. It was a good thing the boy in front of me had new shoes that squeaked so loud when he took a step that everyone on our side of the church laughed as we marched forward which made me happy even though I was sure my spectacles were going to be smashed to smithereens when the bishop knocked them off and we didn't have the money for another pair and I would end up destitute and living in the blackberry thickets by the railroad station with the other hoboes, drinking lighter fluid and eating mice for a living and having only the *New York Post*, a terrible newspaper, for a blanket.

His Excellency was no pixie and he was from the Bronx and he looked like he was eight feet tall and a thousand pounds of muscle when I got within range and got a good look at him. I had seen missionaries before, so I was used to priests not wearing the straightforward black uniform, but I have to say it was unnerving to see a guy who looked like a wrestler wearing bright purple silks and a hat like a huge golden thumbnail. He wore spectacles, which cheered me up for a moment, because no guy with glasses would ever slap another guy with glasses, guys with glasses are like teammates in the dim murk, but then I remembered my brother telling me that His Excellency wore glasses so he could land his slaps with precision, rather than be scattering them all over the place like French artillery officers.

We approached the bishop two by two, as I said, but as we detoured around the altar the lines then merged, so that we approached Slap City boy girl boy girl, and all of this for some reason was in height order, for reasons known only to Sister Marie, who was also a stickler for spacing, so as we climbed the altar and marched ever closer to the bishop we were all discombobulated, trying to keep our spacing right, trying not to think about living on mice and lighter fluid, trying not to laugh at Herman's squeaking shoes, trying to merge properly between glaring girls, and all this on the hottest day anyone could ever remember, despite the brief thunderstorm, which was probably the reason the Mets' pitcher lost his rhythm and ended up walking five Pirates.

The girl in front of me was named Corita and she was one of the tallest girls in class and she had a head of the thickest curliest hair you ever saw, so I couldn't really see what was happening with her and the bishop. I tried to peer around her but she stuck her elbows out angrily and all I could see of His Excellency was the far east and west edges of his purple robes. You never saw anything so purple in your life, and the cloth was some shimmering fabric that reflected light in remarkable ways, so that staring directly at even the edges of the rippling brilliance of his robes was mesmerizing, which is probably the whole point, robewise, when you think about it. Never forget, as my dad likes to say, that the Church Eternal has been around a very long time and it has thought about every tiny detail of the theatrical milieu, and milled it for maximum effect, which you have to admire, as long as you remember it is colorful melodrama, which is to say mannered performance, reflective of substance but not actually, of course, substance itself. This is how my dad talks, which is also mesmerizing.

Finally Corita stepped aside, glaring at me, and I climbed the final step and stood in front of the bishop. He was sitting in the pastor's immense wooden chair, with his crosier in his left hand and his right hand, the slapper, coiled and ready on the arm of the throne. For an instant I got absorbed in his crosier — the crosier is his shepherd's crook, essentially the badge of his office, and to me it looked eerily like a pike or a battle-ax, despite the friendly curls and coils at the top — but then His Excellency leaned in on me and smiled and asked my name. His voice was surprisingly gentle but this too I expected as my brother had told me bishops liked to lull kids before the slap. For another instant I thought about giving him one of my younger brothers' names but then I realized that it was all one and the same to him, another name wouldn't save me, and if I lied to a bishop *on the altar* I would burst into flames and Sister Marie would be upset about spacing.

So I told him my name. He smiled and then, more loudly now, asked me what name I was choosing to bear as a member with full rights and privileges in the Church Eternal. Again I hesitated, and I have to say all these years later that I am still ashamed to say that the first thought that went through my mind was *Bozo!*, but then I said *Patrick!*, as my brothers and I had agreed I would say, and the bishop, his voice now booming, said *Then Patrick I name thee in the Holy Spirit, and I sign thee with the sign of the cross, and confirm thee with the chrism of our salvation in Jesus Christ!* He said this so incredibly loudly that I was sure people a mile away could hear it; he was so loud, in fact, and I was so close to his mouth, that I was shell-shocked for an instant, which is why I lost track of his right hand.

I was never much for peripheral vision anyway, what with the thick spectacles — I have been hit with every sort of ball there is and was once struck a glancing blow by a swallow, which is not a phrase you hear every day — so I didn't see his hand looming until the last possible second. Did I flinch? Sure, I flinched — I mean, I have brothers, and you learn to go with the direction that the blow will carry you, to dilute its force — and as I bent sharply away from his hand, my glasses slipped, and I went for them with both hands; again an unconscious reflex, just like flinching, because there is nothing so important to a guy with glasses as his glasses, without them you are doomed, it's mice and lighter fluid for sure, and as my dad says thank God you are not living in the time of Our Lord Jesus Christ before there *were* such things as glasses, unless you were living in a village through which He passed on His footloose voyages, in which case *you* would be in the New Testament in the place of the woman who touched his cloak, the story changing slightly to be something like *you* touching His cloak and whispering up from the dust a polite request for Him to miraculously invent not one but two pairs of glasses, one as an backup for when you lose the first pair, which we both know will happen.

My brothers told me later there was a titter from the audience at all this, me flinching away and my glasses slipping and all that, but I didn't hear it, for which I am grateful, because I would certainly have burst into tears. Maybe that was a miracle from Our Lord Jesus Christ, to cover my ears for a moment. Or maybe what happened next was a miracle also. I stood up straight, adjusting my glasses, and the bishop's right hand touched me ever so gently, ever so tenderly, on my left cheek, and he said *peace be with you, Patrick, peace be with you,* and he *meant* it, he meant it with all his heart. I could tell that, somehow. I am not kidding and I am not being literary and I mean it as much as I have ever meant anything. I never met that man before that moment and I never met him afterwards, but I tell you true that his eyes were so kind and gentle and merciful and amused that my heart leapt a little even though I was twelve years old and rattled and a little frightened and just beginning to be cynical. He left his huge warm hand on my cheek for another second or two and then he said it again, this time very quietly, just so he and I could hear it, *peace be with you, son, peace be with you,* and I turned away to the west and walked off the altar, and all the rest of my life, until the day I die, I will remember the absolute genuine heartfelt kindness in that man's eyes.

We are always going around looking for miracles and here they are right here waiting patiently for us.

HIS DAD

One day when I was in college, many years ago, and our alarm clock rang at the crack of noon, and I lurched out of the bottom bunk and groggily thumped my roommate in the top bunk. He did not, for once, growl and slide his long legs over the side and leap down hurriedly to beat me to the shower so as to beat me to class, but lay in his bunk, silent and still.

I barked at him and ran for the shower so as to beat him to class but when I got back to our room he had budged not an inch.

This was weird because usually he was the soul of punctuality and he had never cut a class yet, a remarkable thing to say, as some of the young men on our floor had never been to class once, as far as we could tell, despite the fact that intellectual stimulus was ostensibly the product our parents were buying or borrowing for; these young men spent their time playing cards and records and basketball and football, and planning social expeditions and romantic conspiracies, and drinking beer and rum, and arranging dances and dates, and smuggling kegs and paramours into the hall against the rules, and etc. I remember one young man in particular who I do not think ever left the confines of our hall once in the years I lived there. He was thin pale young man with a drawl who said he was from Antarctica. His roommates brought him food, we thought, although no one had ever seen him eat, and there was a rumor that he never slept but prowled the attic in our hall all night long, dreaming of ice.

I asked my roommate if he was sick and he said no, and I asked him if something was broken and he said no, and then he told me that the phone had rung this morning, long before dawn, and that he had leapt down to grab it before I woke, because when the phone rings at four in the morning the news is never good, and indeed the news was bad: his dad had died. It was his mom calling. His dad had been sick but no one expected him to die, but he died, a thousand miles away, suddenly, in his chair on the lawn, the chair with a view of the beach.

I had never cut a class either; I was just as alert as my roommate to the fact that our parents were scratching desperately to send us to college. But I cut class that day. I got dressed and climbed up into the top bunk and sat with my roommate all afternoon. I remember it was a glorious spring day and you could smell flowers and thick redolent plowed soil. Our college was set like Oz amid a vast sea of cornfields and the spring plowing was in full gear and you could smell the dense fat ancient patient soil and imagine it darker than brown, darker than black, composed of creatures that had died and were now preparing to enter creatures that lived.

Other guys came by over the course of the afternoon when they noticed we had missed class, and some guys brought sandwiches, and one guy hopped up in the top bunk with us for a while, which was a kindly thing to do, I thought. Some guys tried to be funny and some guys said religious things but mostly guys understood that just stopping by was enough. A lot of guys stopped by, I have to say. That's what I wanted to tell you about here, that a lot of guys stopped by the top bunk and put a hand on my roommate's shoulder or put a hand gently on his chest as he lay there weeping. That's all. I have been paying attention to prayer and grace for fifty years now, and I don't think I ever saw anything so moving as that.

Finally late in the afternoon I had to go to work in the dining hall, so I jumped down from the top bunk, but another guy said he would take over for me and he climbed up. As I walked down the hall I saw a ragged line of guys waiting to lay a hand on my roommate's shoulder. I have seen a lot of cool things in life, but I never saw anything cooler than that.

THE PROTESTANT

The first Protestant I ever met was a silvery gentleman sitting at a table at my uncle's wedding reception, in New York City, when I was eight years old. This was 1964. I had been the ring-bearer at the wedding, and there had been a tense moment during which I clutched the ring so tightly in my palm that my dad, the best man, had to peel my fingers off it one by one as everyone in the church laughed, and then I had been forced by my mother to waltz with one of the demure flower girls at the reception, during which I thought I would die of embarrassment, so I was already rattled when I was introduced, by my dad, to the Protestant.

The Protestant was sitting alone at a table in the far corner of the reception, near the dessert table, and while now I suppose he was sitting alone because everyone else at his table was dancing or standing outside smoking and talking about the Mets, at that time I assumed he was alone because he was Protestant and no one would sit with him, probably because they didn't speak Protestant.

I had never met a Protestant before, and while I knew they existed, and why they broke away from Our Holy Mother the Church (the Anglicans had to leave because King Henry of England wanted to commit adultery, and the Methodists had to leave because John Wesley made them, and Lutherans had to leave because Martin Luther ruined a church door, and the Presbyterians were Scottish and didn't like anyone telling them what to do), I had never actually met one, so this was a fraught moment, made all the more so because it was my own dad who led me over to him and, talking as easy and friendly as you would to a regular person, introduced us. The Protestant stood and gravely extended his hand and I stood there like a slack-jawed idiot and then my dad said something quietly witty and he and the Protestant laughed and then my dad strode off to do best-man things and I was left alone, for a moment, with the Protestant.

He sat down and gestured for me to sit down which I did, terrified, and he said Now Brian, your father tells me that your great dream is to be a writer, is that right? An ancient and admirable profession, the scribe, the storyteller, the witness.

I was speechless; the Protestant had the same wry erudite tone as my dad! Was this some sort of plot, to get me off my guard so he could lure me to Methodism or something?

I myself am something of a writer, he continued. That is how I came to know and admire your father. We are both journalists, you see — your father for the Catholic press and me for Protestant periodicals. On our side we have the utmost respect for your father. I wonder if you know how esteemed he is in his field, in part because he has reached out to journalists in the other Christian traditions in ways no one in his position has ever done, to my knowledge.

I was still speechless, the very *idea* of being spoken to reasonably by a Protestant being new to me, but by now I had gotten a good look at the man and I saw that he was dressed just like a regular person at a wedding reception, except he had not loosened his tie or imbibed heavily, as yet. His hair was combed, his face was evenly and closely shaved, and he had just the same sort of caterpillar eyebrows as my grandfather. To be wholly honest he looked very much like my grandfather except that he, the Protestant, did not have a pink Racing Form in his pocket, or a diamond tie-pin, or a diamond pinkie-ring like the one Grandfather said was given to him by Divine Providence one afternoon at Belmont Park Race Track.

The Protestant did, however, have a slim silver wedding ring on his left hand, and he must have seen me staring at it, for he said, with some amusement, Are you also married, Brian?

This was such an unusual question that I was moved to speak, and I said no, sir, and he said Although it seems to me that the young lady with whom you danced rather fancied you, but perhaps you did not fancy her quite so much as she fancied you, and I said yes, sir, no, sir, which still seems to me like one of the most bone-headed things I ever said.

Right about then my dad strode back into view and claimed me for Family Photographs but before we left he put both hands on the Protestant's shoulders and said I am deeply touched that you are here, that you made the effort and came all this way. It means a great deal to me. It's the human moments like this that will bring us all back together as a common force for witness and justice, perhaps. It is only history that divides us, and that's all in the past. Think what we might do if we all walk together again.

The Protestant said he too was touched to be invited, and honored, and said You can count on me as a partner in the long work, Jim, and maybe the time will come, when Brian is our age, that the walls have crumbled among the Christian traditions and we are joined in the work we were asked to do by the Founder, and Him a Jewish man at that.

My dad laughed and the Protestant laughed and we parted, but all these years later I remember the way my dad put his hands on that man's shoulders and the way they spoke to each other with real affection and respect and camaraderie. I am older now than they were then, and the walls among the Christian traditions have still not crumbled, for any number of silly reasons mostly having to do with lethargy and money and paranoia, and no sensible person would have the slightest expectation that they will in my lifetime, but sometimes I still wonder what it would be like if they did crumble suddenly somehow and the two billion Christians on earth stood hand in hand, for the first time ever, insisting on mercy and justice and humility and generosity as the real way of the world. You would think that two billion people insisting on something might actually make that thing happen, wouldn't you? And imagine for a moment, just a moment here as we come to the end of the story, what that would be like.

THE OLD GYM

Or here's a wonderful redolent crucial part of our Catholic child-hoods that we do not talk about much and maybe we should: the sweet spicy sharp stinging scent of old gymnasiums in old Catholic schools, with their slightly sagging stages on which the Christmas pageant was held, and commencement exercises, and the annual visit from His Excellency the Bishop; and the side basketball baskets that folded up to the ceiling if necessary and had to be cranked up and down with a pole a thousand feet long that could only be wielded properly by the gruff wizard of a janitor who knew where everything was and could fix everything and could clean up any and all accidents and could if necessary like that one time perform cardiopulmonary resuscitation not to mention temporarily splint broken fingers and ice swollen ankles and soothe Mrs. Adams when she wept uncontrol-lably the day Kennedy was murdered; and the creaking golden dusty wooden floors with their dead spots in the corners toward which sea-soned defenders angled their man in crucial moments of games when you needed a turnover in the worst way such as against the power-houses like Saint Mary Star of the Sea and Saint William the Abbot; and the ancient bathrooms which probably were imported whole and untouched from the catacombs beneath the Eternal City and were dot-ted with heartfelt mosaic messages from the early Christians; and the bleachers which were folded shrieking and groaning back up against the gym wall by dint of tremendous muscular effort from the whole team including even the coach and also as many fathers as could be recruited to push and even that one time Father Pastor although he was older than all the dads put together and rumor had it that he had known Saint Thomas Aquinas personally; and the immense mul-lioned windows which also had to be cranked open with long rusty metal poles and which had not be cleaned since the time Elizabeth Taylor borrowed the church for one of her fifty weddings and the

church and school and rectory and convent were cleaned and repaint-
ed by an anonymous gift from a Welsh actor who married her every
five years or so; and the tremendous doors, each heavier than a hill,
each reportedly made from metal harvested from Luftwaffe airplanes
shot down by members of the parish; and the ancient basketballs,
some as flaccid as towels, which shared the utility closet with rubbery
dodgeballs and moldy softballs and baseballs stained so green with
grass that they looked like fishing floats; and metal folding chairs
stamped with the name of the parish and painted a color never seen
before and never again in the world except on parish folding chairs,
a color something like gray and brown had gotten married and gone
to sea for their honeymoon cruise and both were terribly seasick; and
the occasional sparrow and swallow and even once a crow in the gym,
because the kids would prop the emergency exit doors open to venti-
late the gym knowing that the dramatic signs warning about sirens
and alarms were total fiction; and the stray socks and mathematics
textbooks and love notes beneath the stage, where you could also
find most of the props from the Christmas pageant, not to mention
supplies for May Day and unopened boxes of Baltimore Catechisms
and most of a bottle of Four Roses whiskey; and the two basketball
baskets at each end of the gym floor, one an inch higher than the
other, a fact known to the home team which is why we went that way
in the second halves of games; and the baskets' battered backboards,
once white but now a sort of pearl gray, with the ghostly imprints of
a hundred thousand bad shots stamped faintly on the wood like a
code; and the latticed metal struts that proffered the baskets thirsty
for basketballs; and the silvery nylon nets, never whole for more than
a day, stitched anew to their stalwart loops before every game by a
slight boy sitting on the shoulders of an unsteady burlier boy; and
the two referees, aging and slightly paunchy now but sure of their
authority and quick to issue technical fouls for abuse of equipment
and disrespect of the game; and the squeak and squeal of sneakers
during basketball and volleyball and dodgeball and kickball games,

the last held in the gym only on days of epic and fearsome and inarguable rain; and here at the end of this whopping sentence, the thought occurs to me that the sweetest sound of my Catholic childhood, perhaps the sweetest song and prayer of all because it was so open and innocent and untrammeled and made by and of and for sheer wild headlong joy, was the music of all those sneakers. Remember?

BEST NAPPER OF THE YEAR

On my second day of kindergarten, at a school named for a species of tree, I discovered that our teacher, Miss Appleby, presented a Best Napper Award every week, and that the child who earned the most weekly napping awards was then presented with the Best Napper of the Year Award in June, on the last day of school, in assembly, before the entire school, which went from kindergarten to sixth grade and contained some two hundred students, none of whom, I determined immediately, would outnap *me*.

I report with admirable modesty that I won the first week's Best Napper Award, defeating Michael A., who slept like a rock but flung his feet and fists as he slept (he had six brothers at home). I also won Week Two, in a landslide, but a small moist boy named Brian F. beat me in Week Three, and battle was joined.

We were *all* small, relatively — I mean, this was kindergarten — but Brian F. was especially small; my older brother Kevin, who came to get me one day after school and got a close look at Brian F., said he looked like a wizened gopher — and I felt his size gave him an advantage, in that he could drop down faster to his napping mat and was less likely to be kicked or jostled than someone, say, my size. I appealed to Miss Appleby, on the advice of my older brother Kevin, who said I should ask for a point system or a staggered start or something like that, but she ruled that Brian F. did not have significant or substantive advantage and we went on to Week Four.

It is interesting to note here, by the way, that the girls in our class were terrible nappers; I think a girl won the award only three times in thirty weeks and one of those awards was tainted, I felt, as both Brian F. and I were out sick that week. The winner that week was Margaret O., who couldn't nap if you gave her a cot and a pillow and a quart of gin. My brother Kevin advised me to appeal the award that week but our dad said no, using the word *litigiousness*, which I had never heard before.

Mostly it was Brian F. and me trading awards all through the fall and into winter, although I remember a boy named Michael C. stole the last one before Christmas by egregiously faking his nap, as another boy proved by kicking Michael C. in the ribs, but Miss Appleby did not notice or pretended not to notice; the fact is that Miss Appleby was a sly woman and often pretended not to notice things that no person with eyes and ears could fail to notice, like Margaret O. being a simpering devious sycophant who sucked up to Miss Appleby in the most shocking fashion so as to win Helper of the Week Award and gold stars for her drawings of cats and New York Yankees and the other works of Satan. My brother Kevin just last year told me that he saw a newspaper item on Margaret O. from which the word *probation* leapt out at him, to no one's surprise.

During the Christmas break I worked hard on napping and when school started again in January I went on a tear that I think even now must be the record or close to the record for consecutive napping awards at Birch School. I swept, or slept, right through February before Brian F. recovered his equilibrium and went on a little run of his own, and we opened April tied at seven awards each. With twelve weeks left in the season we were alone at the top, a situation which perhaps rattled us both, as neither of us won the award that month, losing to, in order, Marisa P., who had a cold and was heavily drugged by her mother, Michael A., whose brothers were away at a grandmother's funeral or something, leaving him home alone with his dad, a girl named Gail N., who came out of nowhere that week, like one of those rock bands that makes one unbelievably great song and then never makes a memorable song ever again like Question Mark & The Mysterians, and a girl named Colleen H., who later became a nun in a religious order that worshipped bundles of sticks shaped like canoes according to my brother Kevin, a scholar of these things.

I won the first two weeks of May, Brian F. won the last two weeks in nail-biters (by now there was betting among the boys,

although none of us had any money and we had to bet cookies from our lunches), and with three weeks to go we were again tied. By now even Miss Appleby was caught up in the competition and as June opened she announced that while all of us could and *should* take advantage of Nap Time, she would set aside a corner of the classroom for Brian F. and me to go head to head, as it were — best two of three, for the title.

June that year was powerfully hot and sticky and I remember that we could smell some sort of foul algae stench from a pond nearby and that was one of the summers of the thirteen-year cicada (called, no kidding, *Magicicada*) and the man who mowed the acres of grass around the school went into a manic phase and mowed all day every day so it was harder than usual to drop off thoroughly when Miss Appleby gave the signal; plus there were the murmurs and burbles of the other kids and the faint sound of betting and the sickly whee-dle of Margaret O. sucking up to Miss Appleby and the weird feeling of being within a few inches of Brian F., who was so moist that he sweated aloud and emitted a cloud of humidity so dense that it was a wonder he was not covered with moss and lichen and small ferns.

But if the good sweet Lord ever gave me a gift it is the ability to nap at the drop of a hat and to sleep soundly until roused by gentle mom or loving bride or by a brother with a fist like the knob of a shil-lelagh or by a large dog with truly horrifying breath from recently eating a mole, and I report, again with admirable modesty, that I napped Brian F. *into the ground* over the last three weeks of the sea-son and won the Best Napper Award for June and for the Year and stood before the entire school assembly on the last day of school, in the gym, with the older kids laughing their heads off at me for reasons I did not understand then and spurn happily now. In my view, setting high standards for yourself is a good thing and work-ing toward your goal with all your might is a good thing and how many people can say that they won the Best Napper Award not for a week, like that smarmy insipid Margaret O., or two, like poor twitchy

Michael A., but for a whole *year*? Not so many, I say, with enviable modesty. Not so many.

HER PILLOW

My grandmother lived with us for eight years when I was a child, before she got smaller by the day suddenly and died at the end of a roaring hot summer, as shriveled and withered and bent as the dry rattling plants and bushes around our house. The youngest among us thought she would be buried in the yard and reconstituted by the autumn rains, but this did not happen. Grandmother was grim and happy and equitable and unjust all at once. I begin to think now that I learned a great deal from her about how people really are without realizing I was learning anything. She did not like me or my next brother down and we were forbidden to sit on her reading chair or on her bed. We were forbidden to use her bathroom. We could watch the television in her room only if we were accompanied by our older sister, whom everyone thought was sweet and gentle and everyone wondered how it was that such a sweet and gentle being could be so swiftly obeyed by her rambunctious younger brothers and the secret was a fist in your ear. We were allowed to watch the installation of Pope Paul the Sixth and the funeral of Robert Fitzgerald Kennedy on her television. We were not allowed to watch men walking on the moon on her television because she did not approve of the moon landing and thought it arrogant and specious. She favored our sister because she was the only girl in the house and could be educated properly. Our sister is now a nun in a monastery.

Grandmother favored the youngest among us because he was new and he could be educated properly. He is now president of a high school. But my next brother down and I were older and beyond her reach and she despaired of us and that is why I am a poet. Sometimes she would sigh audibly when the two of us tumbled into view and sometimes she would make tart comments and sometimes she would be goaded to cutting remarks and our mother would say *Mother...* and our grandmother would retire to seethe in her room. She sometimes spent the day seething. I never saw anyone better at being offended. She was Irish. Her room was next to the dining room and if we ate too loudly she would be offended and close her door. I can still hear that door being closed all these years later. One time we tried to throw the youngest among us through her door for complicated reasons and our father who never lost his temper lost his temper and so we learned how to saw and plane and shellac wood. The new door was made of ash and my next brother down is now a master woodworker.

The youngest among us could sit in Grandmother's reading chair and watch television without supervision, and our sister the eventual nun could sit on her bed and touch her photographs of Grandmother's late husband, but not even our sister was allowed under any circumstances whatsoever to touch or recline on her pillow. Her pillow more than anything else smelled like her. Her scent was talcum powder and lavender and rosary beads and butter and rectitude. You could tell where she had been in the house by the trail of her scent as heavy in the air as a song. Her scent was most adamant above her pillow. Perhaps that is why our sister's cat one day curled up on her pillow and delivered three infinitesimally tiny naked horrifying kittens, each one emerging in a sort of moist transparent sandwich bag. My brothers and I watched from a few inches away. The cat patiently licked off the moist guck on the kits and magically their fur appeared. Our grandmother had been at Mass and when she returned she found us in her room with the cat and the kittens huddled on her pillow and it seems to me that everything exploded right after that.

Martin Luther King was murdered and the war got worse and our sister left for college and we had to watch the moon landing on the little television in the family room. Some of our neighbors came over and crowded around the little television with us and because we were little we could hardly see. Grandmother died at the end of that summer and her television came into the family room and the little television went down to the basement woodshop so our father could watch Notre Dame games. Our mother gave away the kittens and the cat was squashed by a car and I don't know what happened to the pillow. I am pretty sure that pillow is long gone from this world, but her scent above it is not gone; as you see.

MY FIRST JESUIT

The first Jesuit I ever met was about eight feet tall and weighed four hundred pounds and his robe alone was so vast that probably it could cover a small state like Delaware if necessary, as another one of us altar boys said, awed.

He wore sandals even though it was stone cold winter when he was visiting our parish to do some sort of secret mysterious spiritual retreat with all the fathers in the Nocturnal Adoration Society. The Nocturnal Adoration Society was a cult that only fathers in the parish could belong to. To be a member of the Society you had to spend one night by yourself adoring the Blessed Sacrament on your knees and smoking cigarettes in the foyer of the church near the photograph of Fulton Sheen, the famous actor. Also you had to drink so much coffee during the night to stay awake to adore the Blessed Sacrament that when you came home at dawn your hands shook as you read the newspaper to see if the blessed Mets had egregiously punted away yet another eminently winnable tilt, as our dad said. Sometimes instead of tilt he said *ostensible contest* or *competitive misadventure* or *theatrical pratfall*. He was not much of a smoker and being in the Nocturnal Adoration Society was harder for him than for the other fathers because they all smoked so continuously and he did not, so he had to take over some of their slots sometimes at night when they had gone ten or twenty minutes without a cigarette and could no longer adore properly. Our dad said he smoked a cigarette once under great duress while in the war, but the foul and vulgar addiction did not establish a beachhead, as he said, and the savings therein may someday pay for an hour of college for one of you children, probably one of the older ones, so far, unless you younger ones make stunning comebacks, like the Mets do once a decade, God help us.

The Jesuit had arrived by train and was picked up by the smallest of the assistant priests, Father Paul, who was the size of a fifth-grader. Father Paul delivered him to the sacristy, as the Jesuit was to celebrate a special early Mass for the fathers in the Nocturnal Adoration Society, and that is how I met him, as I was to be his altar boy. I had just finished cassocking and surplicing when he came into our locker room and sat down companionably. The wooden bench creaked from his weight. We shook hands and went over logistics and then I said shyly that I had never met a Jesuit before and he said Well, there are not so many of us in this country, we are rare birds, you might say, *avibis raris*, and then he laughed so hard that the thin steel locker doors rattled. We are the secret agents of the orders, you might say, he continued. Charged with exploring deeper than what you can see on the surface. Thus our educational urge. But some of us visit parishes. Ostensibly to evangelize but in my case to listen. The real life of the Church is here in the parish. This is why I wish to meet the fathers. Mothers are the greatest teachers of the Word but fathers are only half a step behind. If I can convince the fathers that the Word is not about authority but about humility then perhaps I have done a good thing. Do you have the slightest idea what I am talking about, son?

No, Father.

Any interest in being a Jesuit?

No, Father.

A priest?

No, Father.

Have you ever visited the local seminary?

Yes, Father.

Liked it?

Yes, Father. Glass backboards in the gym. A really beautiful gym.

But then they fed you, is that right?

Yes, Father.

And that was the end of your interest in the priesthood.

Yes, Father.

Ah. Mystery meat and rubber vegetables have done more damage to the Church than any number of Communists. If we had better cooks we could run the world.

Yes, Father.

I wanted to ask him more about himself, about what it was like to be eight feet tall and weigh more than two dads, and what it was like to wear a dress all the time, and if his feet were freezing, but the church was full of impatient dads shaky from coffee and cigarettes all night and Monsignor Stephen the pastor was suddenly there in the doorway glaring at me and reaching solicitously to shake hands with the Jesuit, so he had to go.

A minute later we were lined up by the altar door, Monsignor first and then the Jesuit and then me, and the Jesuit turned around suddenly and whispered, Listen, probably we will not have a chance to talk again, so thanks for your help, and remember this word: *humility*. Will you remember that? Yes? You hold onto that word the rest of your life for me, okay? It's the great secret to everything. It's the key that unlocks all problems and puzzles. Ask your dad about it. He'll know what I mean.

Yes, Father, I whispered, and Monsignor turned and glared at me and then he gave the signal to process and we processed and that was that; after Mass the Jesuit was hustled away for discussions and disquisitions and dinners and I never saw him again. I never did catch his name either and even my brothers who remember everything cannot remember his name, although most of my brothers also remember that he was bigger than any professional wrestler or football player we ever saw and it probably took ten men ten months to sew that man's robe, as my youngest brother said.

I told my dad this story a while ago, when we were reminiscing about the Nocturnal Adoration Society and the Ladies' Altar Sodality and the Third Order of Saint Francis and other agencies of our life in our parish long ago, and he said he vividly remembered that spiritual retreat with the Jesuit and remembered some of the other fathers saying it was a disappointment, partly because there was no golf and beer, but partly too because all the Jesuit talked about was what we could surrender of our illusory authority and wisdom, said my dad. Many of the other fathers were bored and some were even annoyed, he said, but a few of us heard something piercing that we never forgot. People assume they know what the Jesuits are like, but I suspect there is a great deal more to the Jesuits than we see. If that man is any example of how they think and conduct their vowed lives, then I conclude they are wise because they know they aren't. And you have to give that man credit as a retreat leader — here it is all these years later and both you and I remember what it was he asked us to remember, about humility. Now *that* is an effective retreat master, to have something said forty years ago still be shining in the front of your mind, isn't that so?

HIS GENIUS

If you are like me, which God forbid such a sorry penance, you find yourself contemplating That or Whom which we call God (for lack of a better label) on a regular basis, and I do not mean church on Sunday. I mean daily, thrice daily, five times daily and twice at night, because you know, down under sense and logic and reason, that there is a Singing, a Breathing, a Mercy beyond accounting under and through all things; and you wish to love and thank Whatever or Whomever this is; and, in fact, if you are honest with yourself, you find that you no longer wish to be granted favors, as you did when you were young, but rather you wish quietly to put your small gifts in harness to Whomever's agenda, because you know now, after fifty years, that it is all about love and that is why we are here and life is short and you had better work as hard as you can for love, which is another word for That or Whom.

You contemplate Him (for lack of a better pronoun) with awe, amusement, fury, gratitude, despair, confusion, applause. You question His existence and His agenda and His goals and objectives. You would very much like to see a copy of His mission statement and detailed future plans, with footnotes and documentation, ideally notarized. You regularly conclude that His ultimate genius is the inarguable seething miracle of creation — He is the greatest Author ever, even better than Flannery O'Connor, whom He, of course, invented — and you admire the fact that only once has He directly claimed authorship of everything that is, when He lost His temper three thousand years ago and roared **WAST THOU THERE WHEN I LAID THE FOUNDATIONS OF THE EARTH?!** at poor old furunculated Job.

But lately I have been contemplating an even subtler and more devious aspect of His genius: the fact that He adamantly and deftly refuses to appear in public, except by reflection and intimation, and except perhaps somehow, miraculously, in some weird way we poor muddles will never understand, in perfect corporeal and spiritual synchronicity with a thin Judean carpenter's apprentice a thousand years after He popped a gasket with poor old ragged Job, and roared **WHO LAID THE CORNER STONE THEREOF WHEN THE MORNING STARS SANG TOGETHER?!**, and poor Job covered with ash did quake and shiver in the dust, and was silent and agape.

Even in the olden times He did not appear whole and inarguable, but spake from a burning bush, thundering **I AM WHO AM** at poor Moses, which even now many years after I first heard and read it seems like the coolest tautology ever.

But never did Moses nor Job see Him; and even those thousands of eyes that perceived the thin Judean and walked with him on hill and dell and gazed upon him as he spoke to the multitudes and saw him dimly weeping in the garden and contemplated his sagging corpse on the cross and saw him upon the road to Emmaus or finally in the room on the second floor with its doors locked and bolted did not see Whomever, but instead saw a slight brown human being in whom Whomever was resident, or infused, or concomitant; nor did all the millions of people over thousands of years who saw a Light, a Force, a Sign, see Whomever, but rather a flash or hint or messenger from Him; as did the thousands of people who saw and heard the woman once called Miryam, always cloaked in blue and radiant and serene, often smiling, when she appears in woods and hills and speaks to children and farmers; she is from Him but not Him, or Whatever, or Whomever; words and labels for the Mercy being ever weaker the more we seek after Him and how to bend our work to His agenda.

Behind the scenes, hidden and elusive, a wild ragged figure flitting from tree to tree, motioning to us, as Flannery O'Connor wrote, but never quite perceptible; how brilliant and subtle, to *not* be evident and inarguable; what genius! For of course by all sense and reason and logic we must then conclude that there is no God, there has never been God, there cannot be God; in fact the evidence is everywhere against the engine of love and mercy for which we use the word God, as we see from the daily deluge of pain and loss and murder and rape and greed and theft.

So our heads are sure that there is no God; but our hearts are not. They yearn, and psychologists say that we yearn for mother and security; they yearn, and the cocksure say that faith is fiction and religion a childish joke; and yet we yearn.

But if we saw Him clear we would not yearn; and this is genius. If He spoke to us clear, if He laid His starry hand upon our perspirant brows, we would be awed and thrilled, but we would not yearn; and this is genius, that He hideth from us and will not be seen, and so we yearn and doubt and must cut our own paths through the thickets.

We would not do the work if we thought He would do it for us; and this is genius, that our work *is* Him.

Suffice it to say that if He appeared before me this minute, at the kitchen table, three feet away, sitting where the youngest son usually sits, as you can tell from the crumbs in little drifts in the tablecloth, I would cover mine old eyes, behind their glittering spectacles, and ask Him politely to be gone and again be a terrible and generous mystery, the most extraordinary Absence I can imagine; and this is His genius, which I sing this morning, covered with bread crumbs, silent and agape, as the stars sing together and the coffee is almost ready; and so amen.

II.

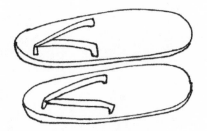

A SORT OF CHAPEL

My dad took the train into New York City for his work as a journalist, which meant that usually he took the 5:25 train home from work, except for the occasional night when he and my mom would stay in the city for dinner or a play (an event twice followed, nine months later, by a new brother); but there was one night that he did not come home, because he got stuck under the East River in a Long Island Rail Road train for seven hours, courtesy of the Great Blackout of 1965. By the time the power came back on and the train was hauled back into Pennsylvania Station, it was past midnight and my dad ended up sleeping in the 34th Street Armory, home of the 71st Regiment of the United States Army. Although he had been a sergeant in the Second World War and a lieutenant during the Korean War, he slept on the floor, rather than ask for a cot.

I asked him about that night recently and he said the first thing that happened when the lights flickered off and the train groaned to a halt was a wonderful silence that went on for ten or twenty minutes easy. I suppose it was partly composed of shock and trepidation, he says, but there was also something of wonder in it. I doubt any one of us on the train that evening had been in such a silent crowded darkness but once or twice in life and here we all were, crowded together, no one moving, and not a word or a sound. It was like we were in a sort of chapel. There was emergency lighting, so we were not in complete darkness, and a few people had transistor radios, so we soon heard about the blackout.

Then there was a period of...disgruntlement, says Dad. Complaints and accusations and imprecations. All natural enough, but unpleasant. Also quiet fear — was this an attack by an enemy? There were people who were genuinely frightened and claustrophobic. You felt badly for them. For all we knew we were now trapped under the river for days, and who had food? What about hygiene, water, a place to sleep? Sure, we all thought about that. In my car there was a young woman who was terribly frightened. But again I think of a chapel because people turned to her and were warm and kind. People switched seats so that women could sit with her and calm her with their voices. As if she was their own daughter and their voices could soothe her somehow. I was impressed by that gesture. Similarly there was a man who was very upset, and other men quietly surrounded him, in case of trouble.

After a couple of hours it seemed evident that we might be stuck under the river for quite some time, and people began to make subtle adjustments. I remember that apples were shared. There was a man who offered to lead us in prayer but no one seemed very interested and that effort came to naught. One poor fellow very much had to answer the call of nature and with great embarrassment I believe he did, in a corner, but no one said anything. I remember that people looked away and did not insult or excoriate him. I think this was a kindness. The poor fellow was very embarrassed. He wore a long coat, I remember, and he huddled inside it the rest of the night.

Most people slept or dozed after a while. It was very quiet and to be honest it was essentially peaceful, or restful. This was in November and it had been a cold day in the city, but down under the river we were all crowded together in our car so it grew quite warm. Most people fell asleep. I dozed on and off. At one point there was a flicker of light and we thought the power was coming back but it vanished and we were in the dimness again. I do remember that in that instant of light I saw many people asleep with their heads resting on their neighbor's shoulders. Even now this is a cheering image to me. Everyone thinks that New Yorkers are tough and rude and violent but we are actually not, so much. Faced with troubles we reach for each other like anyone else. I suppose that's the image I remember best from that night, people leaning on each other and no one shrugging anyone else off angrily. Again I think of a chapel, in which people sit shoulder to shoulder, gentle and calm, waiting for light.

When the lights finally came back on after seven hours there was a cheer, and then when the train began to move there was another cheer, although we were moving backwards, and soon we were up out of the river and back into Pennsylvania Station again. We all walked up onto the street to discover that the city was, of course, quite dark, although there was a brilliant full moon. It was quiet, but not silent; there were cars abroad and policemen on every other street just to be sure order was kept, and the bars were all open — while they could not pull beer, they could serve liquor. I walked down to 27th Street, thinking I would sleep in my office, but the building was locked, so I walked back uptown to the Armory and found room on the floor and fell asleep under my overcoat. In the morning I called your mother and took the train home.

I remember that next morning, I tell my dad. I remember it well. It was a school day, but Mom let us stay home to wait for you to come home. There were all of us children at home still, in 1965; this was before we began to launch one by one into the world, never to return, and we waited on the porch for you to turn the corner and stroll down our street with your fedora hat and your quiet smile and your overcoat flapping. Mom stood with us, holding the baby.

In the summer when our father turned the corner the three youngest of us would jump off the porch and run down the street to greet him and hold his hands and carry his briefcase, but when the weather was grim we would huddle on the porch and wait for him, and this seems to me now to be a sort of chapel also. We stood together shoulder to shoulder, no one jostling or elbowing anyone else angrily, and waited for our father, and when he leapt up the stairs of the porch we opened like a sea to welcome him home with great joy.

MY BROTHER PETER

One of my children (we have three, but two of them are twins and they move so fast I have never been completely sure who is whom) said recently, *you hardly ever write about growing up with Unca Peter*. So let me redress this problem and tell you about my brother Peter, who is about six feet twelve inches tall and weighs probably thirty pounds, although you never met a stronger skinny guy in your life; it's like he's made out of steel wire, complete with a vast Snidely Whiplash mustache. When Peter got annoyed as a boy he would extend his pterodactyl arms and pin you to the wall like a poster, and there you would remain, struggling ineffectually, until his favorite television show came on. This was *The Wild Wild West*, with Robert Conrad and his sidekick Ross Martin, and it wasn't on until just after dinnertime, so I spent many an afternoon tattooed to the wall by a guy taller than a tree with arms as long as the Strait of Hormuz. Sometimes, during those long drowsy hours, during which I used to imagine the novels I would someday write, I had the impression that he was nailing me to the wall with merely two of his long bony spidery fingers, also made out of adamant steel, while he read our Silver Surfer comics with his other hand, but this was before I got spectacles and discovered that the world was arranged in sharp edges, rather than being the most amazing series of inchoate shapes, some of which were nuns and automobiles and brothers and one time a surfboard apparently going back upstream to spawn.

As Peter and I were only a year apart in age, we were brought up essentially as twins, wearing the same sailor suits and saddle shoes when young and affecting the same denim jackets and surly attitudes as teenagers and sentenced to the same crewcuts for our first twelve years because our dad liked the way we looked like walking peaches, but our interests diverged early. I fell headlong into books, and Peter into the wilderness; he grew immensely tall, while I did not; he developed astounding skills with wood, which he understood like a language, while I grew adept only with a typewriter; I adored basketball, while he devoted his thousands of athletic hours to frisbee, at which he was wonderful; he climbed mountains and strode through forests and kayaked rivers, while I swam in the dim shadowed alleys of cities, coming only as close to a forest as the pages of my books could remember their ancestry. He went west and I stayed east; he married young and I waited long for love; he lives in the mountains and I live near the sea.

For many years it seemed to me that there was an edge between us, an edge I did not understand, as for many years I assumed much about my family without peering overmuch beneath the hood; and for many years I winced and bristled at his teasing, rising easily to the bait and wondering afterwards at the etiology of my annoyance. Then, slowly, I began to realize that like many men we spoke in codes and ciphers, at oblique angles, in part perhaps because we were shy, in part because love is a muddle, in part because often what seems jest is joust; and I realized too that most of what we wanted to say to each other could not finally be shaped into words.

For any number of reasons we all wear masks of various style and character and, even as pain and humility and mercy and hard wisdom peel them away, some remain, molded forever to the shape of your face; so that when we most want to say *I love you, I love you more than I can say, I love you more than words know yet,* we are sentenced to forcing awkward squawk through the holes in our masks. Of course what emerges is not what we intended; of course it is often misunderstood; of course what was born warm seems cool or cold after its long voyage. How ironic to have to say this, after fifty years of utter absorption in the magic and music of words; but they are weak vessels, easily swamped; which is perhaps the prime reason languages are always changing and morphing and stealing from each other, in a desperate effort to evolve into something that finally fits the twist of our tongues to the depths of our hearts.

But this is speculation for linguists and mystics. I wanted to tell you about my brother Peter, and so I have spoken of his great height and endless arms, the sprawl of his mustache and the welter of his skills, his thirst for high places and open air, but I have not said the thing I most wanted to say to him, unadorned and for once unmasked: *I love you, I love you more than I can say, I love you more than words know yet.* It may well be that words are weak, and hardly ever do they do more than suggest and intimate that which we wish to sing, to shout; but words are what we have to hand to each other, and this morning those are the words I hand to you, brother.

HOW TO LOVE YOUR NEIGHBOR
WHO IS A ROARING IDIOT
OR EVEN WORSE

Aw, it's easy to love Mr. C., as he's the guy who cheerfully lends his tools to everyone on the street and gives away hatfuls of fresh redolent summer savory tomatoes, and he's the kind of guy who has an extra set of tire chains in his garage for when you have to suddenly drive over the mountain to retrieve a sick kid from college, and he says *ah keep em until spring it's not like I need them, son.* It's easy to love *that* guy.

It's not as easy to love Mrs. M., who is a ferocious bitter snide supercilious gossip and loves to intimate that easy drugs and easier sex are rife among the teenagery in the neighborhood. But it can be done, if you just smile and grind your teeth and consider that at least she is not heavily armed, or the governor, or in charge of the national twitter feed.

And it's just stone-cold *not* easy to love the guy down the street who parks all his huge vehicles in front of everyone else's house, and was caught once dumping motor oil in the creek, and more than once has spent the night passed out cold in the moonscape of his garden. But you endure him, and you say hey when you pass him in the street, and you talk a little sports, on the general theory that any flash of humanity might cool him out and maybe make him stop parking his starfleet vehicles in front of tiny Mrs. H.'s cottage.

But what about slimebags like Mr. Osama bin Laden, who murdered three of my friends twelve years ago this morning? What about a neighbor like that? Because he *was* my neighbor, damn it, as much as I wish he was resident on Venus. That man roasted children on the airplanes. He fomented the murder of many thousands of his fellow Muslims. How can I love a preening twisted coward like that guy?

Because if I cannot even try then I am a liar when it comes to being Catholic. Because if I cannot find it in me to believe, reluctantly and furiously and disgruntledly and raging against it all the way, that there was some shard of holiness in even that scum, some flash of I Am Who Am, some breath of the Unimaginable One, then to say I am Catholic is a foul lie.

We *say* we believe all living things are holy. We *say* we believe there is The Christ in every heart — Christ-in-us, as Saint Paul says. We *say* we believe that He is not dead but resident in each and every person born of woman in this bruised and blessed world, a miracle.

But if the mysterious Word is alive in every heart, then He was in some chamber of even bin Laden's, and Hitler's, and Mao's, and Stalin's, and the endless parade of thugs that fill our newspapers and smartphones and history with their shrill crowing lies.

What?! Criminals! Murderers! Their souls roast in hells fired by the eternal fuel of their evil egos!

Probably. But if you and I cannot believe that God made even them, breathed His love into their hearts as infants, gave them their chance to sing and share the Gift, then we are shameful liars. *That* is what Catholicism demands. It is about love, period. It is not about easy love. That is the revolution of it, the incredible illogical unreasonable genius of it. It is about loving those you hate and would happily imprison or execute. It is about knowing that they are you brothers and you are not at all unlike them, with murderous splinters in your own heart. It is about being honest.

Listen: it is terribly, daily, hourly, immensely difficult for me to believe that there was a shred of decency in the man who murdered my friends Tommy Crotty, Farrell Lynch, and Sean Lynch. It is as close to impossible today, September 11, 2013. But I am damn well going to try, because I don't think Mr. Jesus Christ was a liar, and I think what He said is the only thing that can save the world, and us, and my beloved children, and yours.

Amen.

THE BRIDES OF JESUS

The morning that my cousin entered the convent all the parents and older kids were sentenced to the reception in the church hall, but us lesser kids were allowed to roam free which we did among bushes fat with roses. We were on a hill so high that plowed fields down below were the size of postage stamps. There were hawks circling above us in the convent garden, and we told our littlest cousins the hawks were angels with orange tails. Our uncle stepped out of the reception to smoke a cigarette. He is the father of the bride of Christ. When you become a nun you marry Christ and wear His ring but you never kiss him or go for a ride in his car and then have babies later like our other girl cousins did. Christ had no children because He died young like the young fireman who was going to marry another cousin but the burning house fell on him and his casket was closed because all that was left of him was an ember. That cousin cries whenever we have barbecues and that is why. Angels have colored tails depending on what country they came from before they were made angels.

When our uncle was finished with his cigarette he gestured irritably at us and we all went to the chapel for the wedding of our cousin to Jesus.

There were three other girls getting married to Jesus that day and they wore white also. One of them was the most beautiful girl you ever saw. Maybe she was an actress whose star has fallen, said an aunt. A fallen woman is one who goes for a ride in a car without a wedding ring. Some angels have black tails because they were from Communist countries. Our cousin was not the most beautiful girl you ever saw, which she said herself, laughing, which is part of the reason we loved her so. Another uncle said our cousin had to be a nun because no one else would marry her except Jesus, and Him a Jewish boy! Our mother said this was a snide sneering supercilious stupid remark and our father said that is an excellent example of alliteration.

Our uncle the father of the bride did not sit down in the front pew with the other parents but instead walked back and forth in the back of the chapel, stepping outside every few minutes to smoke another cigarette. Halfway through the ceremony when there was a long period of contemplative prayer our father got up and walked outside to retrieve our uncle. The chapel was so quiet you could hear the hawks calling to each other in their own angelic language. Every being has its own language and only a few human beings have ever been able to understand all languages, the most recent being Thomas Merton. Angels speak their own private language which is composed of music too beautiful for us to comprehend. Our father found our uncle weeping so hard he did not have the heart to haul him back inside but instead stood with him outside for the remainder of the ceremony. When a man is weeping it is the task of his friend to stand with him silently in commiseration. That is what men do.

When the ceremony was over we all walked outside and our aunt glared at our uncle but he did not quail and we all lined up in two burbling jostling rows. The brides of Jesus walked through us glowing and now they wore veils of a color far beyond white. Angels are depicted wearing white but that is only because our printing processes cannot approximate the color that they actually wear, which is far beyond our understanding. The first three brides of Jesus walked with their eyes cast down in demure fashion, but as our cousin came through she held out both hands and we all reached to touch her like after a basketball game and her mother our aunt was brave and did not weep but her father our uncle wept copiously. Just before the convent gate clanged shut behind the four brides, our cousin turned and waved and she was laughing. She was always smiling and laughing which was part of the reason we loved her so. Then we all went to eat, but our dad had to drive our uncle the father of the bride because he was in no condition to drive at all whatsoever.

MR. HILLERMAN

I had the pleasure, some years ago, of having dinner with the late Tony Hillerman, of New Mexico, and that long gentle vernal evening comes back to me now in cheerful memory, for not only was he the most genial and attentive and unarrogant of famous authors but his wife, Marie, was even cooler, as is so very often the case with writers of the male persuasion. Some hours of riveting and fascinating conversation passed, in which the Hillermans were astounded by my alluring bride and we were delighted by the wry genuine honest unadorned brains of the Hillermans and, as Mr. Hillerman said, it was a good thing that he did not have to stand and deliver remarks, for he would much prefer to sit comfortably and have a second beer and continue to talk about books and deserts and the Dineh people of the southwestern United States and his days as a Catholic schoolboy in Oklahoma and his service in the war. He had been an infantryman, he said, a regular old grunt; only later did I discover that he had won two medals for courage under fire and a Purple Heart for incurring damages and that his knees and eye didn't work right because he had been blown up by the Nazis.

He talked about his love for newspapers (he had worked for papers and wire services in Texas and Oklahoma and then been editor of the Santa Fe *New Mexican*). He talked about teaching at the University of New Mexico, which he did for a long time. He and Marie talked with great high glee about their children. He talked about how she was way smarter than he was, and she talked about how she had helped him become a novelist by saying do it and this was when they had six little kids and hardly a penny.

We talked about how the essay might be the coolest form of all and how he loved writing essays but hardly ever made the time, to his regret, and how novels grow on their own once you have written enough for the characters to take over. We talked about other American writers we admired, most of all Twain and Willa Cather, who if all she ever wrote was *Death Comes for the Archbishop* that would have been masterpieces enough for one writer, said Mr. Hillerman.

We talked about how history is stories and research is asking questions about stories and how novels are really collections of stories about the same characters. We talked about how you can always be leaner in your writing and the first rule is indeed slay your darlings. We talked about the Navajo, and he said you could spend ten lifetimes listening to stories from the Dineh and never hear but a small percentage of all the Navajo stories there are. We talked about how a lot of writing is just trying to catch and share stories before the stories vanish for one reason or another. We talked about being Catholic and how the deepest way to be Catholic was to not take religion seriously but to take spirituality very seriously indeed. We talked about how writing was spiritual in nature when it was witness and how witness was really the final gift and responsibility and accomplishment of the writer once you realized that it wasn't all about you.

Right about there, Mrs. Hillerman said she thought that humility and mercy and kindness were the final frontiers for human beings to achieve and Mr. Hillerman said see, this sort of remark was proof that Marie was smarter than he was, and then we talked about the joy and chaos and hilarity and tension of children, and then, the dinner being at the university where I work, other people began coming over to shake hands and have their photographs taken with Mr. Hillerman and the cheerful intimacy of our dinner ended, but I have never forgotten how unarrogant that man was, how warm and friendly and unadorned, how unimpressed with fame and plaudits, how in love with his wife he was, how happy he was to be himself, unpretentious and unpretending. History will remember the wonderful writer, one of the best to sing the West; but I remember the man who, when I asked him his greatest feat, said, Why, asking Marie to marry me!

THE FRONT SEATS

In the first row first seat at Saint John's there was a girl named Colleen who was the smartest kid in the class and always got the best grades and never punted a test even once. One time she got a 94 instead of 100 and she burst into tears right there in class. She was scrawny and did not talk much and had pimples and her dad had cheated people and gone to jail. Her mother came to pick her up every day in a car that smoked and groaned. Her little brother was in first grade and one time a second-grade kid teased him in the playground saying your father was a jailbird and the little kid broke the bigger kid's nose. You would be surprised how much blood there was. There was blood all over and the bigger kid cried so hard that other kids nearby began to cry also. Our teacher dragged the bigger kid to the school nurse. I remember that was the week we played Saint Mary Star of the Sea and lost by only twelve points. Our coach said this was a moral victory. A moral victory is when you lose by twenty points or less.

In the second row first seat there was a boy named Mike who was Italian and did not speak much either because he had an accent. His father was so short that some of the kids in our class were taller than he was. Mike's father was one of the four men who brought the collection baskets around in church and he was so short that when he extended the basket down a pew with its long handle you couldn't see him so it looked like the basket had appeared magically by itself in the air which was totally possible because the world was filled with miracles. That is what our faith is all about, said our teacher. There are miracles everywhere and you must train your eyes to see them. Each and every one of you is a miracle if only you had the eyes to see. You can see miracles more clearly if your heart is pure. Our faith is like a set of spectacles with which to see better. If your vision was terrible and you had the chance to wear glasses to see better, would you refuse to wear glasses? No, of course not. And yet there are people who refuse this divine gift. We must pray that their hearts are opened and the beams of timber are lifted from their eyes.

In the third row first seat there was a girl named Marisa. She was very fat. She later became an actress in a terrible movie that you could only see on television once a year late at night before the screen went to mush and the television station played America the Beautiful. I think it may have won an award as the worst movie of all time, but Marisa was good in it. Her part was to be a waitress handing a man a cup of coffee. She didn't spill a single drop of that coffee. She was on screen for four whole seconds but for those four seconds you totally believed she was a waitress in a diner in New York serving coffee to a detective rather than the girl who used to be fat in the third row first seat. She was so believable that you suddenly wanted a cup of coffee even if you didn't drink coffee and couldn't stand the taste of coffee and could not conceive what lunatic in ancient times decided to roast beans from a bush and call it delicious.

In the fourth row first seat there was a girl named Patricia. She was the first girl to have breasts of all the girls in our class. One week she was like the other girls and the next week she had breasts. At the end of the first week she had breasts our teacher asked her to stay after class and the next week Patricia wore a sweater over her shirt. Sometimes she would take her sweater off in the playground when she and the other girls were running and we boys would stop playing basketball for a while and when she put her sweater back on the game would resume. The first week Patricia had breasts was the week we beat both Saint Barnabas and Saint William the Abbot, neither of which we had beaten since the dawn of recorded time, and Saint William the Abbot had a terrific center who later went on to play college ball.

In the fifth and final row first seat there was a slight boy named Matthew who had behavioral problems. He could not sit still under any circumstances whatsoever and he muttered and talked to himself and laughed at inopportune times. Supposedly his mother cut his hair with a hunting knife. His house was filled with brothers and dogs and drugs. If you went to his house to do a science project you had to watch out for dog poop on the floor and on the stairs and even in his room. Even when he was talking to you his eyes went sideways, so people who had never talked to him were always looking sideways to see what he was looking at. He used to sit in the back of the room with the other cool kids, but our teacher finally assigned him his seat fifth row first seat for the rest of the year no matter what and if he sat anywhere else she would stop teaching and point to his seat and he would shuffle up the row touching people's hair and talking to himself. He never wore socks even in winter and sometimes he would wear shoes that did not match. Sometimes he signed his papers with other names than his own and sometimes when we were in the playground he made us call him Timmy or Jimmy. One time he bit another kid in the playground and our teacher came to take him to the principal and he held back, crying, and suddenly our teacher began to cry also. They stood there looking at each other and crying and crying. We all stood around silently and no one moved and finally our teacher reached out and put her hand on his head as gently as you would touch a broken bird and then she turned and walked away without bringing him to the principal at all. I remember that was the week we lost to Saint Agnes, which was no surprise, as we had lost to Saint Agnes every year since Jesus was a child in Judea long ago.

DRIVING TO COLLEGE

The little towns where you got off at the first exit ostensibly for gas and coffee and to see a man about the purchase of a horse but found yourself driving slowly under the towering arch of the elms on Main Street First Street Broad Street Elm Street and noticing the leaves scuffling and dervishing in the silvery yawn of dawn and slowly driving past a sleepy citizen thrashing his coat pockets for the key to open the diner the gas station the coffee shop and you roll the window down for that extraordinary ordinary magical wet cold loamy metallic sweet redolent American *scent* and the guy sleeping just behind you mutters in his sleep and you roll your window back up, but not all the way, because he who drives is king.

All the other guys in the car are sound asleep making noises like old halting stuttering motors and you are not totally sure which United State you are in but you guess you might be halfway to school, maybe closer. It's someone else's turn to drive and you really should get gas but you keep driving though the town because just as you think you should stop for gas and coffee all the streetlights blink off except one which fizzles and stammers for a bit and then dies with a soft startled pop! and for some reason this makes you keep driving.

You cruise down a street of small shaggy wooden houses most of them sagging just a bit as comfortably as old college couches and it seems like every third house has a light on in the kitchen and if you drive slowly enough you will surely see a man in his bathrobe shuffling out for the newspaper which is not in the mailbox but on the second step of his porch because the paperboy threw it from his old bicycle without stopping and didn't get any juice on the throw; and just before you turn back west again, there is the man, bending for the paper. His bathrobe is exactly like the painting of Joseph's Coat of Many Colors in the Illustrated Bible for Children and you think of your mom and the way her long fingers lovingly flittered the pages and you would happily have sat wedged into her sweet powdery gentle smell for a thousand years but you grew up and went to college which is totally fine and good and great and the right thing; but still.

At the edge of town you drive along gazing into the hills dense with beech and oak and maple and there is a tattered mist in the folds and ripples of the woods and you hear the first cautious caw of crow just as a state trooper goes by headed in the other direction. You watch him in your mirror and he is watching you in his and you have the usual flutter of trepidation but then he lifts his right hand just enough for you to see he is saying *hey* and not *pull over*, so you lift your hand also and signal *hey* and think confusedly for a few minutes about being American.

To get back to the highway you have to pass slowly back through town under the elms on Main Street First Street Broad Street Elm Street, and this time half the storefronts have lights on, and as you go past the diner you see a young man in work boots holding the door open for an old woman in rubber boots and somehow that puts you back on the highway, as your buddies sleep like rocks like stones like college students, and for the next few silent moments as you drive you are in the diner, eating two scrambled eggs with fried potatoes and bacon and toast, and the waitress with her hair pinned up like a bird's nest gives you a whole *pot* of coffee and a jar of honey shaped liked a bear, and when you ask for the newspapers she says something tart and wry to the cook and a minute later she gives you not only today's paper but the sports sections from the last two days, and on the radio very faintly you hear there will be snow by late afternoon, first flurries and then, along midnight, two to four inches, with winds up to ten miles an hour from the southeast. News is next. Remember: deer season opens in two weeks.

MY FIRST ORDINATION

My first date with the sweet wild woman who eventually married me was as follows: We drove two hundred miles from Boston, at speeds exceeding the speed limit, because as usual we started late, and also because someone forgot her dress, which entailed retrieving it again at shocking rates of speed, and we screeched to a stop three hours later at a taxi stand in New York City, beneath a sign that said NO PARKING AT ANY TIME, and we sprinted, yes, sprinted, to a church, one of us making shockingly loud noises with her high heels on the pavement, and arrived breathless at the ordination at the exact moment that the subject of the ordination, my friend Tom, was sprawled facedown on the cold stone floor of the aisle of the church as everyone in the church chanted the Litany of the Saints.

I will continue with this essay in a moment but I think we should pause and admire this last sentence, which I cannot believe was ever written before in any language.

Technically we were just in time for the actual moment of ordination, the Laying On of Hands, when the bishop cups the candidate's head like a coconut and prays silently that the Holy Spirit will infuse this man with the joy of the Lord's work and the humility necessary to achieve it, with courage against duress and with unrelenting faith in the mercy of the One upon us all; but we had, to my dismay, missed a lot of the cool parts of the ordination already, parts which I knew about because my friend Tom had told me about them with high glee and anticipation: the gathering of the candidates on the steps of the church, and the last hurried cigarette before becoming a priest for the rest of your life, and afterwards too; the Calling of the Candidates after opening prayers, during which the bishop basically takes attendance and makes sure no man slept in late or got married the night before or bagged out altogether so as not to miss the Knicks game; the Presentation and Inquiry, during which the bishop (who as you see does all the work during an ordination), asks for some witness that the men before him are worthy of the rare and astounding sacrament they are about to receive; the Acceptance, during which the bishop, probably sweating a little by now, as it was a wicked hot day, says okay, we will accept these men as candidates for the priesthood, which usually gets a roar of applause from the relieved parents and family members and former girlfriends in attendance; the Promise of Obedience, during which the bishop holds hands with each candidate and looks him grimly in the eye and essentially makes it clear that while yes, an informed conscience is the final moral arbiter according to the canon laws of Our Mother the Church, he, the bishop, is the ward boss of record and don't you forget it, at which point the candidate, if he is wise, says something like *I do so swear.*

My friend Tom, with whom I had gone to school since we were six, said he was going to say *I do so declare!* in honor of the words we had to write on so many examination papers at Saint John Vianney Grade School, but I don't know if he did.

My date at the ordination by now had caught her breath and was curious which of the prostrate ordinands was my friend Tom, whom she had never met, and I pointed him out; Tom was easily identifiable by his sort-of-mohawk haircut, which he had adopted for reasons that elude me. It was rare then and now to see a candidate for the priesthood with a mohawk, but I remember with a smile Tom's reply to people who questioned his sanity: *at least it's not a mullet, for God's sake,* which was true.

Just then the Chanting of the Litany concluded and the ordinands stood up and I caught Tom's eye and he grinned and said hey man and then he went back to being ordained, although not before casting an appraising eye over my date, whom he had never met. We talked about that glance after his ordination and I said courteously that if he stared at her again like that I would shave his mohawk with a butter knife, and he said *aw, think of it this way, she is the very last stunning woman I saw as a bachelor before swearing to God and man that I would be a temple of the Lord forever,* which is a good point.

Then came the Laying On of Hands, which made many among the congregation smile, for you hardly ever see a bishop clutching a mohawk, but after the general amusement there was, I have to say, a few moments of haunting silence and emotional power, during which I sensed for the first time the incredibly deep throbbing holiness of the ancient ritual. After the bishop lay his hands on the heads of the ordinands, every other priest in attendance did so also, in total silence, and I confess that I nearly wept, it was so sweet and sad and joyous all at once; you saw, for an instant, The Priesthood, in all its muddled glory; mere men, of all shapes and sizes and haircuts, fat and thin, short and tall, pink and brown and white, bald and hirsute, lined up along the rail, the older ones reaching with real tenderness and reverence to cup the faces of the younger ones and pray from the bottoms of their hearts for these men that they not fail their vows, or lose their faith, or be possessed by greed and avarice, but rather serve the faithful with every iota of their beings, and bring the revolutionary message of the Christ to every corner of the world, and finally be taken back home to the light of the Lord, Who would be well pleased with His servant and reward him with a place in the front rank of the Elect.

One of the many reasons I think I fell in love with the woman who would eventually be my wife was that when I turned to whisper something of my feelings at that moment I found her sobbing silently. Of course I did not have a handkerchief to offer, being an idiot, but she used the shoulder of my suit jacket, a gesture which still seems to me unutterably sexy.

After the Laying On of the Hands comes the Vesting, during which the new priest, no longer an ordinand, removes the stole he has been wearing, which is a deacon's stole, and is handed a new stole, which is a priest's stole, and a chasuble, which is the cloth like a cloak or a poncho that a priest wears when he is in full battle rattle, as my friend Tom later called his new regalia. This too was a sweet moment because the older priests helped the younger priests into their new battle rattle and there was a lot of laughing and chaffing on both sides about fit and drapery and such. Then there was the Anointing of the Hands with oil, after which each new pair of hands were wrapped in pristine cloth for a moment, and then all the new priests and the older priests and the bishop celebrated Mass together. The new priests all made a point of offering the consecrated bread and wine to the congregation and of course each family and friend and former girlfriend of the new priest went to their own boy for Communion, which made me nearly weep again, for you never saw mothers so thrilled and bereft, or fathers so proud and trying not to think of grandchildren, or former girlfriends so confused and moved.

After Communion I thought that was the end of all the possible cool parts of an ordination but how wrong I was, for the very last part, it turns out, is that the *bishop* now kneels down and all the new priests one by one cup *his* head, and ask for blessings on their ward boss, which seems like a very fair and equitable state of affairs to me, for we are all muddles in search of miracles, no matter what hat we wear.

Then the new priests lined up together on the altar steps and they all blessed the congregation together at once, which was sweet and funny, as they were by no means in sync, and there was a roar of applause and lots of camera flashes, and that was the end of the ordination. As the new priests filed down the aisle following the bishop they extended their hands to the congregation and more than a few of them stopped for a moment to hug their mothers, who were weeping copiously.

There was a reception after that in the church basement and then there were lots of dinner parties and such for the new priests, but the woman who would eventually be my wife and I had to hit the road, so we went down to the basement to see Tom, who was glowing. His mom and his sister and his aunt were there, and while they fawned over the woman who would eventually be my wife, Tom and I had a moment to talk about his dad, who had died young, and who would have been awfully proud. He would have hated the mohawk something fierce, said Tom, but he would have been awfully happy. In fact he *is* awfully happy. One great thing about being a priest is that you can use present tense with authority when you talk about stuff like that, you know what I mean? I said I did know what he meant, and he offered to celebrate my wedding to the woman who would eventually be my wife when and if she lost her mind and acceded to my proposal, and I report with great pleasure that this actually came to pass, two years later, in Oregon, on the most beautiful May afternoon you ever saw.

III.

THE CAP

My brother died a year ago, and in that year people have asked me, here and there, always tenderly, always with real interest, which is a sweet gift, *what do you miss most about him?*

And for a while I would say things like his false gruffness, or the way his stern glare would suddenly give way to a shy smile like sun through a hedge, or the way no man on earth ever loved making sandwiches in the kitchen as much as he did, and nobody over the age of eight more enjoyed a glass of milk with his sandwich either; but now I find myself saying things like the way his mustache was bristling and adamant under the prow of his nose, or the way his hair would *not* stay combed even though the man was in his sixties for heaven's sake, or the way his shoes as big as boats waited for him in the slanting sunlight of the mudroom of his house where hung also his caps and hats, and do we ever think about what a worn familiar old cap might feel, having lost the head that loved it for thirty years? Do we? If *you* were a worn familiar lovely old Irish cap, and you had waited anxiously all night every night for thirty years for the blessing of the morning when he would reach for you and knead you with real affection and something almost like reverence for the way you sheltered his tumultuous head for thirty years and then fold you gently over his ungovernable hair and down over the prow of his nose and away with the two of ye into the wind and the rain, voyaging across campus and through the woods and around the town until the moment when he stepped back into the mudroom and removed you and shook the holy water from you and hung you again on the poke of your peg, wouldn't you wonder where he was the first few days after he vanished and then feel something like a silent sadness and wonder if he would ever again knead you and don you and doff you and reach for you with real affection and something almost like reverence?

We are so sure that we are the only ones who feel things, but how very wrong we might well be.

His pens and pencils and notebooks; his vast collections and volumes and pressings of stamps and coins; his favorite socks and ratty shirts; the scissors molded by the years to the heft of his hand; his spectacles and his belts, his binoculars and bird books; the chairs that knew his weight and wondered as that weight steadily declined, until by the end when he sank into them they thought they held a long child and not a burly man; I think of these things now when people ask me what I miss about my brother.

Many an essay, and greater ones too, can be written about the wife and daughter and son he loved, and the grandson he will never meet, now, the grandson named for him, the grandson with the same long-lipped face as his son, the grandson to whom he might well have presented his beloved cap one day when the boy reached for it, curious but a good three feet shy of the peg; but right there is a good place to stop, with my brother kneading his cap with affection and draping it on his grandson, the two of them laughing, the cap surprised and then delighted, and then away with the three of ye, voyaging into the wind and the rain.

WE DID

Did we punch and hammer and jab each other as children thrashing and rambling, a large family in a small house filled with brothers and one older sister with sharp bony fists and no reluctance to use them?

We did.

Did we use implements like long whippy maple branches and our mom's bamboo garden poles and our dad's old sagging tennis rackets and redolent pieces of oozy lumber stolen from the new house going up down the block and brick chips and new sharp-edged asbestos shingles torn off the garage roof as ammunition and weaponry with which to battle and joust with brothers and occasionally the Murphy boys next door, each one burlier and angrier and Irisher than the one below him?

We did.

Did we occasionally use snowballs meticulously packed as tight as possible and then placed carefully in the freezer for hours or days as stony ammunition and rocklike weaponry despite the cold hard fact that said snowballs should have been registered with the United Nations especially the time one of us saved a few *until June* and hammered the Murphy boys in the most lopsided glorious victory of all time on our street?

We did.

Did our mother actually say more than once *you will put your eye out!* and finally we bought individual glass eyes at a sale from the estate of an ophthalmologist and faked a terrific raucous brawl so that our mother came running only to find her sons roaring about their lost eyes which were bouncing and rolling freely on the linoleum floor which caused our blessed mother to shriek which caused our calm large muscular father to come running which caused the collective entirety of his sons to spend many hours in penitential labor and one of us had to go to confession as the mastermind?

We did.

Did we play football so hard in the yard that more than once one brother's helmet went flying and more than once a finger was broken and one time tempers flared such that a picket from the old red picket fence was used for assault and battery?

We did.

Did we play basketball so intently and furiously that more than once a nose broke and eyeglasses broke and teeth were chipped and skin was abraded and ankles rolled and fouls were delivered with violent intent which was repaid in full in the fullness of time?

We did.

Did we many times wrestle our oldest tallest brother to the ground, often using our youngest brother as a missile aimed at his feet to get him off balance and, once the tree was toppled, jump upon him with cheerful violent alacrity and pile on with as much emphasis as humanly possible, sometimes jumping off the couch to cannonball down upon him, while ignoring the plaintive murmur of our youngest brother trapped at the bottom of the pile, mewling like a new kitten?

We did.

Did we occasionally reach or lurch or lunge across the table during meals to commit crimes upon the bodies of our brothers even though our dad had said and he meant it too that the next boy who reached across the table with bad intent would lose a finger?

We did.

We did these things, all these things, and more things too, and you would think the accumulated violence would brood dislike, or bitterness, or vengeful urges, but I report with amazement that it did not. Yes, the trundle of years and the fading of memory is at play here. Yes, we are all much older and slower and have lost the language of pummel and lash. Yes, we have all witnessed and endured pain and loss in such doses that the thrash and crash of our brotherly years seems minor now compared to the larger darkness.

But there is something else here; in some strange way, in some way I don't understand, our crashing and tackling and wrestling was about love. Maybe we did not have words then for what we felt and had to use our sharp elbows and long whippy maple branches as halting stammering tongues. Maybe our apprentice years at love were always rough and bruising. Maybe we were trying to say something gentle when we were ungentle.

Maybe we use our hands to say things when we have no words for the things we want so desperately to say. That is what I have tried to do with my hands this morning, brothers. Remember the crash of bodies and the grapple in the grass and the laughing pile on the rug, for that was the thrum of our love, brothers. So now let us arise and haul our youngest brother out from the bottom of the pile by his thin flailing legs and restore him to a semblance of his usual shape and volume and proceed to dinner, laughing and chaffing and shouldering, and it will always be this moment somehow, brothers, just before dinner, just before the tide of time rises, in the instant of silence just before our dad says grace.

מִרְיָם

I see Her everywhere. How could that be, considering she lived twenty
centuries ago and by all logic and reason should be no more than
dust motes and scraps of legend? Yet I see and feel and hear Her. Not
on tortillas and stop signs and glowing above fields and forests. No:
in gestures and instants and tones of music and color, somehow. This
makes no sense, but I know it is Her, and my sensible friends sneer
and laugh and accuse me of dreaming and I smile and nod and know
it is Her in ways no one will ever understand. She is in us and aware
of us and graces us and does not rest or quit. She knows who we are
and what we are capable of. She is not the Formative Imagination but
She is of Him. She is not the One Made Flesh but She is of Him also.
She is not the Proximate Spark, that which we call the Spirit for lack
of a better word, but She is infused by and an exemplar of That also.
So many useless pronouns and awed capital letters for that which we
know is true but can never explain; and of its aspects She is the one I
hold closest to my heart, for I have seen her in my small sinewy bowed
tough smiling mother, and in the brave wild woman who married
me, and in our lean quiet daughter, sometimes, especially when she
was small; and I have seen Her in the way people touch each other
gently in order to speak without words; I have been aware of Her in
moments of epic mercy and pain and grace; I know Her to be patient
and enduring and calm and as refreshing as rain after drought; I once
heard Her speak to me in the secret caverns of my mind in the middle
of the night when I was as filled with despair as I have ever been or
hope to be; I know that She does walk back into our world sometimes, and speaks to children and farmers, and whispers to them in
words made of light. We'll never understand how this could be so, but
deep down in our bones we know it is so, don't we?

Reach beyond intellect and admit it silently as we stand huddled and awed in this sentence. She is not a metaphor; She is not an avatar for feminine spiritual energy; She is not an icon, a symbol, a figure we invent to use as focus: She *is*. There is no conceivable way that could be so. Yet once there was a girl named Miryam, מִרְיָם in the language of Her people, a name that may mean *strong waters* or *my love*; and She lived in this world of pain and joy, and some say She rose into the sky beyond the sight of mortals rather than shrivel and die as the rest of us must; but here She is on this page, and in our hearts, and somehow, beyond sense and reason, standing behind you. If you don't use your eyes you will see Her.

VISITATION DAY

Here's a small thing that isn't. As usual, as always. A father and his daughter are strolling across the campus where I work. It's Visitation Day — the last day before new students either enroll here or decide to go elsewhere, the poor things. So the campus this morning is filled with students and their parents and sometimes grandparents and they are all walking in every direction toward every sort of informational meeting imaginable. It's all beautifully meticulously planned and paced and there is excellent signage and there are tall confident friendly current students acting as guides and ambassadors and the campus is glowing in the sudden sunlight, partly because the groundskeepers spent the previous week begging the roses and dogwoods to bloom and editing scraggly bushes and laying down redolent bark dust and erecting bright new banners and persuading the ground squirrels to take a day off from mating in small wriggling knots on the main quadrangle.

The university where I work is a Catholic university, so we dearly love the title Visitation Day because we think that Mary the Mother of Jesus has a wry sense of humor and when She is apprised of the date of our Visitation Day She will smile and clear Her calendar and decide to visit, probably registering Her Son in the humanities, although there are those of us who think of Him more as an engineer or an entrepreneur. One of us annually puts in for a special parking pass for Her and Her Son in front of the gym where the opening informational motivational session starring the president is held, but we never actually granted Her a pass, which may be why She has not yet come for Visitation Day, that we know.

The father and the daughter in the opening paragraph of this essay are actually heading directly toward our sweet lovely bronze statue of Mary the Mother of Jesus, which stands at the nexus of several pathways so that no matter how you are cutting across the quadrangle you must pass pretty close by Her left hand, which is held out in greeting or blessing to passersby, and many is the time I have seen someone scurrying past lean toward Her and brush their fingers against Her fingers, which always moves me deeply and has more than once made me weep, for murky reasons. Also I have seen students place notes in Her hand, and I have seen a man holding Her hand while praying with his head bowed so low I bet his neck was sore for days, and twice now I have seen Her hand filled with snow.

As the daughter walked with her father she twice danced all around him so smoothly and gracefully that he never broke stride but only smiled, and then, just before they got to Mary the Mother of Jesus, the daughter, now back in stride with her dad, reached for his hand, and he took her hand, and for another few steps they walked hand in hand, just like they must have done when she was a tiny girl, although now she was a tall woman. By now they were only a few steps from Mary but I never did see if either or both of them reached for Her fingers because I was standing in the redolent bark dust under the oak trees weeping yet again. You would think a man long past age fifty would be able to explain or at least try to explain why a young woman reaching for her father's hand so gently like that would set me to watering the oaks, but I haven't the faintest idea. Perhaps it was the sharp stinging scent of the bark dust in my eyes. Perhaps it was because my daughter is a woman now and we used to walk hand in hand when she was tiny and when we did I was so happy there are no words for how happy I was. Perhaps because it is always Visitation Day in this bruised blessed world and when we reach for each other in the sudden sunlight we are also somehow reaching for Her. That could be. That could certainly be.

IV.

A SONG FOR NURSES

The first time I saw a nurse was when I was four years old and some-one cut my tonsils out and I woke up addled to find a cheerful woman wearing white leaning over me and murmuring something gentle. The room was all white and the bed was all white and there were white curtains framing the window. I thought I had died and was in heaven and the woman leaning over me was an angel. I was deeply relieved to be in heaven because I had recently sinned grievously and my brother still had a black eye. For a moment I wondered if the woman smiling at me was the Madonna, but then I remembered the Madonna wore blue.

The woman leaning over me then said gently *everything will be all right,* which it was, after a while, during which I discovered that I was not yet dead and that she was a nurse. But for me ever since nurs-es are essentially angelic, and even now that I am deep into my fifties and have lived long and seen much, I have never yet been disabused of the notion that nurses are gentle and witty and brilliant and holy beings who bring light and peace, even though I know they must have dark nights when they are weary and sad and thrashed by despair like a beach by a tide.

I have seen nurses help bring my children out of the sea of their mother and into the sharp and bracing air of this world. I have seen nurses praying by my tiny son's bed before and after his heart was edited so that he could live to be a lanky and testy teenager today. I have seen nurses grappling cheerfully with the wires and coils and tubes and plugs and buttons and toggles and keyboards of vast machinery beyond my ken. I have seen nurses with blood on their blouses in the nether reaches of the night in emergency rooms. I have seen nurses hold my children's heads as my children were sick upon their shoes, and never a snarl did I hear from those nurses but only a soothing sound deep in the throats, a sound far more ancient than any civilization. I have heard friends of mine who are nurses speak eloquently and articulately about their work as witness, as story-saving, as patience and endurance, as being those souls who stand by the door between life and death and usher other people through it in both directions. I have quietly gaped in awe at the sinewy courage and flinty strength and oceanic grace of nurses, and many times considered what our hospitals and hospices and clinics and schools and lives would be without them; which is to say starker and colder and more brittle and fearful. We would be even more alone and scared than we are now when faced with pain and confusion.

We take them for granted, yes we do. We think of them with reverence and gratitude only when we see them briskly and gently at work, leaning over us and those we love, being both tart and sweet at once; but here, this morning, let us pause a moment and pray for them in the holy cave of our mouths and thank the Mercy for these most able and skillful agents of His dream for us: that we will rise to love and joy, that we will achieve humility, that we will shape our humor and labor and creativity into lives that are prayers in motion, prayers applied to salve and solve the pain of our companions on the road. Let us, in short, pray not only for the extraordinary smiling armies of nurses among us; let us pray to *be* like them: sinewy and tender, gracious and honest, avatars of love.

SIX STORIES

In all the years I have known all the priests I have ever known, not one has ever violated the sanctity of the confessional, to my knowledge; which is a remarkable and refreshing sentence, when you think about it, because privacy in matters of spiritual tumult is a basic and essential tenet of our faith. Yet over the years I have heard many riveting stories of things said to priests while the priests and the tellers of the tales were *not* formally engaged in the sacrament of reconciliation, and I repeat some of these in amazement, because they are funny and poignant, and taken collectively they say something about how sweet and weird and complicated we are as a species. To wit:

- The theft of one used tire, which immediately exploded upon first use by the thief, which the thief took to be a direct and unequivocal sign from the Mercy. The thief returned the tire to the original owner. The priest who told me this story said he asked the man why he would return a ruined tire, and the thief said, with some surprise, because it *wasn't my tire,* Father, aren't you paying attention?

- The admission of assault (but *not* battery) upon a squirrel (*Sciurus griseu,* the western grey or silver squirrel), by a homeowner, occasioned by what the homeowner characterized as "continual deliberate provocation" by the squirrel in question, upon which the homeowner's temper finally snapped and he did roar at, threaten, insult, denigrate, and impugn the squirrel in question, for which the homeowner felt awful, three days later.

- The theft of a copy of *Milton's Paradise Lost* from a college bookstore, to use as source text for a paper due the next morning. When the student's paper earned an F, on account of egregious plagiarism, the student destroyed the book, on account of John Milton being directly responsible for the F.

- Running up the score in a Catholic Youth Organization sixth-grade basketball game because Coach B, the coach of the losing team, had once dated and rudely dumped Coach A's wife, long before Coach A and his wife had married, but Coach A had never forgotten the way his wife was hurt by the awkward end of that previous relationship, and he, Coach A, given the sudden opportunity for vengeance, could not help himself, and even when his team was up by 24 points early in the second half, told his team to apply a full-court press against the other team for the rest of the game, for which he, Coach A, felt guilty the next day and sought a conversation with a priest. When the priest asked him if he would like to confess, he (Coach A) said well, no, we only won by 32, that's not a sin, Father — winning by 50 would be a sin.

- The theft and secret delivery to Goodwill of a woman's white go-go boots by her long-time boyfriend, who told the priest he just could not *stand* to see them in the closet any more, after eight long years of seeing those tacky things leering at me when I opened the closet every morning and evening, that's like *6,000* forced sightings of those awful boots, Father, she never wore them once, and she would never throw them out or give them away, even though *she never wore them once* and said many times she would *never ever wear them again* as they were associated with some unpleasant memory, but she would *never give them away,* Father, even though I all but begged her to do so, and finally I just couldn't take it anymore. The priest said politely that this didn't seem like such a bad thing, really, just a little contretemps that could be smoothed over by an honest talk, and the man said well, that's the problem, Father. I blamed it on the dog, and now she wants me to take the dog to the vet to make sure she, the dog, has passed everything successfully and there might even be those little shoe nails in the heels of the boots, like cobblers use, which could cause serious intestinal distress, and a visit to the vet costs a hundred dollars *just for the visit,* let alone x-rays and a thorough interior examination, which might require anesthesia. Once you get into anesthesia you are talking serious money.

I should probably stop here, because it's so tempting to leave you with the image of this earnest fellow staring anxiously at the gentle priest, hoping for some pastoral wisdom, as the priest tries desperately not to burst out howling with laughter (he told me that it was such a near thing he thought he sprained his face trying not to laugh), but another priest friend of mine told me a story the other day about a woman who finally snapped after *twenty consecutive mornings* of finding her daily newspaper in a wet huddle in the street *right below the mailbox,* how hard would it have been for the delivery person to place it in the dry mailbox rather than just *drop it in the street,* how hard is that!?, after which she waited by the mailbox on the 21st morning and when a battered car drove by slowly and an arm extended and her newspaper flew out and landed in the street she shrieked and cursed and shouted; but then when the car stopped and backed up jerkily she saw the driver, a sleepy elderly man wearing a worn baseball cap, and she suddenly felt terrible and selfish and arrogant. In this case, when the priest asked the person telling the story if she would like the sacrament of reconciliation, she said yes, Father, she would, for thoughtlessness of that scope was a sin, she thought, and she would like to ask the Creator for forgiveness for being so chippy about such a small thing and being so rude to someone who very probably had a much harder life than she did.

BAPTISM: A NOTE

Few of us remember our own baptisms, as we were utterly concentrated on other matters then, like milk, and trying not to tip over helplessly to gales of laughter when your brothers propped you up on the couch and made bets on how fast you would tip over because you had a head like Russia on a body like Belgium. But I have eyewitnesses to my baptism, eyewitnesses I trust implicitly, and they tell me I was anointed with oil and splashed by water and draped in a glowing white gown that sure looked like a tiny wedding dress and by Grandmother's handmade lace doily which she reserved for special occasions like Robert Emmet's birthday (March 4) and the day Oliver Cromwell died and descended into Hell (September 3).

My oldest brother Kevin was fond of telling me all sorts of stories about my baptism, one of which included a brawl among our cousins, and many of which included me urinating copiously, and one which featured me spitting and kicking in a suspicious manner when the priest made the Sign of the Cross on my forehead, and *what* a forehead you had then, said my brother, it was like the blessed north face of the Eiger in the Swiss Alps, it went on for *weeks,* a party of eight explorers and their pack horses could have gotten lost on your forehead to never be found again despite diligent search by upstanding members of the community. It's a good thing you eventually grew hair. You had the biggest head anyone had ever seen when you were born, you know. Dad used to sell tickets to people who wanted to see your head for themselves, on Saturdays. You wouldn't believe how many people would line up to see your head.

Sometimes my brother said so many babies were to be baptized on the same day I was baptized that the priest christened us with numbers instead of names, to speed things up a little and make parish recording easier, and so actually my name is Nine. Other times he said I was mixed up with a girl baby and I was actually christened

Maureen but he then would say he could not tell me anything more about that incident for legal reasons and I should not ask Mom because she will get upset and start cursing in Gaelic again and Dad says *grandmother* cursing in Gaelic every day is *plenty* of people cursing in Gaelic in *this* house, in his considered opinion.

Sometimes my brother said *he* was baptized by Fulton Sheen, who was passing through New York City on his many peregrinations on behalf of Fulton Sheen, and sometimes he says he was baptized by Teilhard de Chardin, who actually was in residence in New York City at that time, arguing with the Church authorities who had banned the promulgation of all his amazing and confusing books, and sometimes he said he was baptized by Mom in an emergency during a snowstorm, which actually is quite possible, as there was a terrific snowstorm in New York City the day he was born, in February 1948, and any person of good intention can indeed baptize a child by saying "I baptize you in the name of the Father and the Son and the Holy Spirit" and pouring water over the head of the child. My other brothers and I have asked our mom if she indeed baptized our oldest brother Kevin in a snowstorm, but the word *snowstorm* sets her off about not being able to *get a taxi* when you would *think* by God a taxi would be *available*, the whole *point* of taxis being *availability in times of extreme weather*, especially when the person hailing a taxi is *visibly and egregiously pregnant*, but no, there were *no taxis to be had* and she and my dad had to walk from Mass to the hospital, *twelve whole blocks*, in a roaring *blizzard*, and you *bet* the Mayor at the time, one William O'Dwyer, from County Mayo *to boot*, heard about this later from herself, and you would think he would be looking out for *his own* instead of gallivanting around the city not attending to *taxi service*, God help us all.

HAUNTING FRIDAY

On Good Friday every year, which seemed terribly named to me and ought to be called Bleak Friday or Haunting Friday or Be Silent & Remember Friday, I sit in the balcony of the campus chapel, behind a whopping oaken pillar so no one will be distracted when I weep copiously, and I weep copiously at the sheer human pain and grace of the whole thing.

From the first moment when the priest walks up the aisle and then for once does not wander around behind the altar but startlingly prostrates himself with his face hidden, his robe spread over him like the plumage of an enormous broken bird; to Christ murmuring *I thirst!* and Peter ashamed by the fire and poor Malchus bending down to pick up his ear; to the freighted moment when everyone kneels silently with the image of that actual broken brave exhausted young man dying seconds ago on a dark afternoon — the ceremony is the most emotionally naked and honest day of the Christian year, the day we stare suffering in the face, the day we stare at the brave broken young man as He tumultuously was, not the remote legendary hero we so often reduce him to.

I am annually moved to tears by this communal honesty, by our crowded silence, by the creak and thud of our knees on the shining wooden floor of the chapel, by the shiver and ring of voices in the dark corners as they tell the story again for the millionth time in the long history of the churches that grew from that freighted awful obscure epic moment.

And every year now I know that there will be a line, a glance, that catches me by surprise and hits me amidships; and this year there were two.

First, old prickly thorny testy brilliant Isaiah: "...there were many who were appalled at him — his appearance so disfigured...his form marred...He had no beauty or majesty to attract us to him, nothing in his appearance that we should desire him...He was despised and rejected by mankind, a man of suffering, and familiar with pain. Like one from whom people hide their faces he was despised, and we held him in low esteem...He was oppressed and afflicted, yet he did not open his mouth...He was assigned a grave with the wicked... though he had done no violence, nor was any deceit in his mouth..."

I sat there, behind the huge oaken pillar, gaping just like the gaping kings in this tale from thousands of years ago, because maybe for the first time I really *heard* what was being said, I heard it deep and true and piercing: He was us! He is us! Ugly and bruised and ignored, nothing in our appearance to occasion desire, familiar with pain and held in low esteem, battered and tattered; and yet we do not complain but forge on ahead one step at a time...That's us! That's the vast oceanic majority of us, who are neither twisted murderers nor perfect agents of love but muddled mixes of greed and glory, sin and courage, reverence and ruin, laziness and light! How apt and right and perfect that the Creator, poured into the skin of a young brown man during the reign of Gaius Octavius, would be neither handsome nor rich, charming nor muscular, famous nor wealthy; a regular joe, a man you would never pick out of a crowd, although you might well finger Him in a police lineup. Adamant inarguable astonishing genius: us! As ragged and decent and testy and frightened and weary and thirsty and haunted and brave as any one of us is, or can be, daily. Not a superstar, not a hero, not a glorious shining being, but a thin confusing irascible young man, beaten by the cops and hung out to die.

I sat there for long moments, as the Passion ended and the Veneration began, and I was moved, and I was grateful for the vision, and I expected none else, for one epiphany a day is a lot of epiphany; but then *another* vision came to me and I was grateful for it, for it set my heart to sing, and perhaps it will set yours singing also.

A girl, maybe age seven; tall for her age, with plaited pigtails and a blue checkered dress; walking toward the cross with her mother behind her, her mother carrying the baby; and I watched them approach, wondering idly if the girl was just along with her mother from curiosity, or if she would nod at the cross, or even perhaps bend and touch it like everyone else; but then when her turn came she suddenly stepped forward eagerly, and knelt, and wrapped her arms around the cross, and hugged it tight, as tight as she would her mother or father or brother, as tight as she would hug someone she loved and trusted with all her perfect unbroken heart, and I could see even from the balcony that her eyes were closed and her face was lit with a smile you could see from Saturn.

Maybe she knelt there transfixed and transported for six seconds, or eight, or ten, and then she disentangled herself and jumped up and stepped aside and waited for her mother, who held the baby with her left arm and touched the cross with her right; but to me it seemed an hour, a year, that this sweet holy brilliant girl held that poor bruised young man in her arms and gave Him her love and sent me smiling back out into the light, my face shining and my heart singing; and now perhaps yours too. And so, Amen.

HOW TO HIT YOUR DAD

A friend of mine is talking about his father. His father beat him up about every other day when he was little. Usually just weekdays, though, he says. Usually we took the weekend off. Weekdays he would stop in the bar on the way home from work and then come looking for me. I was the oldest and I figured, well, better me than my kid brothers. I understood the whole Christ thing early on. It never occurred to me when I was little that there was a world in which dads did not come home from the bar and beat up their oldest sons. It was totally normal, you know what I mean? It was so normal I used to wish I had been born later in the family so I didn't have to get beat up all the time. It wasn't until I was about ten that I understood that my dad was different from most other dads.

I got good at being beat up. I learned defense. How to huddle, how to protect your face, how to lean back or sideways at the right time to reduce the blow, you know? Later when I had boxing lessons I realized I had taught myself instinctively how to accept a punch. I got good at using my forearms to catch a blow, so he would feel like he got me, that his punch landed, but it would be mostly just banging on my forearms. Never broke a bone, though. I started hitting back at about age twelve. I remember the first time I hit him back. He was shocked. I hit him in the stomach as hard as I could. He was real surprised. He came back strong though. Angrier than before. He was pretty much always angry. I never knew why. After that I learned how to just keep him *engaged* until he ran out of gas, you know? *I learned how to hit my dad,* isn't that a weird sentence? I learned how to keep him from getting his feet set. That was important. A punch where a guy just gets the power from his arm doesn't hurt as much as one where he gets his legs into it. I got good at jabs and feints and keeping him off-balance. It turned into sort of a waiting game. He'd start strong and then I would just wear him out. He'd run out of gas after about ten minutes. He would just walk away silently. He never said anything, no. I figured it was good that he didn't yell and curse. He was just a hitter. I used to wonder if he didn't want to have kids and I was living proof that he had kids.

My mom never said anything about it and after he was dead there wasn't much call to talk about it, I guess. I turned out to be relatively normal myself, so what is there to talk about? Now it all just seems weird and sad. I didn't get to know him well, which is sad. I don't know why he was a hitter. He just was. He only hit my kid brothers once or twice. I thought about teaching them how to hit our dad, but I figured better they didn't know until they had to know, right? For a long time I felt weird because I didn't *feel* anything about this. I wasn't angry. I just wanted to age out of the program. I figured he would stop when I got bigger than him, which is basically what happened, plus I went into the Army.

I worried about myself when we had our first son, but he's a great kid and I turned out to be a regular dad — *what* a relief. I was really worried. My wife understood. She's great like that. She's never pushed me to try to figure out my dad, either, which I appreciate. It's just sad, is all. I'll never know what kind of dad he would have been if he wasn't a hitter. Sometimes when he wore out he would just suddenly stop and there would be like five seconds where we would just stand there and I always wished he would *say* something right then, you know what I mean? Like that was our chance. But he never said anything and then he would walk away. Probably those few seconds are where he could have started to be a regular dad and we could have worked out something, but it never happened, and now he's dead, so what can you do? I think about him a lot now that I am a dad trying to be a good dad. Maybe he wanted to be a regular dad but he just could never find a way to get there. I feel almost bad for him sometimes. Almost.

CONGRESS

The first time I ever heard sex discussed in class was in seventh grade, and it was a particularly interesting discussion because the word sex never appeared, nor did any other word you might think would surface in a discussion of sex. No, the discussion centered on the word *congress,* and it all started because Mr. Kelly told us that his wife was pregnant; and he must have been sleep-deprived or addled by joy, because he started the conversation about sex himself, by saying that *pregnancy was necessarily preceded by congress,* which confused everyone in class, even the sniggering boys in the back who were sniggering to cover the fact that they hadn't the slightest idea what he was talking about.

There was then a brief puzzling discussion of how the United States Senate and House of Representatives could cause pregnancy (with seed projects, one girl said), a discussion I still remember with pleasure for the way that Dougie Manning's mouth fell open like a startled trout, but then Mr. Kelly barked at the sniggering boys so sharply that one of them lost his spectacles and, to his eternal credit, Mr. Kelly then did his level best to tell us something that he thought we ought to know about our bodies and our prospective love lives, without using words and phrases that he knew might well get him fired from our school named for a saint and run by a monsignor who had, in the local paper, called *The Sound of Music* 'prurient trash,' a phrase my father dearly loved and used for years afterwards at every opportunity.

I would guess that Mr. Kelly spent a solid twenty minutes with us that day, struggling to convey to us something of the sweet surge of desire, not unlike the rising of sap in spring, and the inarticulate joy of mutual surrender, and the intricate sculpture and pleasure of intimate grapple, and the way that congress is anciently a haven for our vigorous lonely spirits, and the way time retreats and huddles forgotten in a corner until the moment you lie weary and thrilled in each other's' arms and count yourself as fully awake and attuned and alive as any being on the earth in that moment, and the quiet secret anticipation of life sparked inside your wife, and the inchoate sensation of lying awake late at night as she sleeps, fitfully, near the end of her term, and the way you watch as the hands and feet and knobby skull of your son or daughter slide by inside the womb of the woman you love and how ever so gently, so as not to wake your lovely bride, you touch the hand or foot or crown of your mysterious magical miraculous child, who somehow amazingly *feels your touch also* through the scrim of skin that temporarily separates you, and you lie back smiling in the marital bed, and dream of the child you have never met but will very soon, God willing.

I remember the word *inchoate* in Mr. Kelly's speech, because I looked it up later, and I remember the way that the sniggering stopped, and the abashed laughter faded, and we sat rapt; not so much, I think, at the titillation of the subject as at the teller of the tale; for Mr. Kelly was tough, he was stern, he was gruff, he was the Man Teacher in a faculty otherwise all female and mostly veiled; but this one day we saw beneath his somber mask, and I bet none of us ever really forgot the way his talk became not at all a lesson but a confession, an elegy, a poem, a song. I suspect now that he may have taught us more about something that day than he or we ever gave him credit for; for he taught us, gently, obliquely, carefully, sweetly, that lust was at its best when it was the servant of love — a lesson I sometimes think is being forgotten a little bit every day, which is more than a shame and something very like a sin.

SO VERY MUCH THE BEST OF US

One day in elementary school a boy in the playground punched a nun in the belly. His name was Billy and her name was Sister Marie. It was an accident. She had come running to break up a fight and Billy had swung at his opponent with his eyes closed because the other boy was bigger and older and Billy was scared and Sister had tossed the other boy out of the way like a leaf just as Billy's fist arrived where her womb was. She gasped and doubled over and Billy opened his eyes and burst into tears. This was shocking because Billy was burly and we had never seen him cry even when the bigger older boy had punched him so savagely in the shoulder that Billy had a bruise for a month which I can attest to because he and I played shirts and skins basketball and I saw it snarl under his skin and change colors and slowly die like a painful memory.

Sister was only bent double for a few seconds but in those few seconds her veil slipped forward so that when she stood up again it fell off. A boy named Kevin picked it up and handed it to her. We all stared at her crewcut. Nobody said anything. There was dust on Sister's veil, I remember that. She seemed to be crying. Billy was still crying also. The bigger older boy tried to edge away but a few smaller boys grabbed him and held on. Sister told him to report to the principal this very minute and then she said to Billy you come with me young man and they went off together, Sister with her arm on his shoulders like he was her little brother and she was his sister and they were going to the Mets game or something. Her veil was unbalanced so she looked jaunty or weekendish, as our dad said of people who wore their hats cocked or askew or awry. Our dad wore a fedora hat to work in the city during the week but never on the weekend because, he said, hats were forms of disguise or costumery and there was no need to caper or indulge in vapid theatrics on the weekend and, besides, Jesus Christ Himself never wore a hat on the weekend so why should he?

Years later I was having tea one morning with my mom and dad and I told them about this moment in the playground and my mother said That poor child, and I said Oh, Billy recovered right quick and ended up being a fireman for the city, and she said No, no, I mean Sister Marie and not the violence but the veil, to have lost that even for a moment before you children was to have lost something crucial. Poor child. She would have been in her twenties, you know. Still creating herself. Still trying to be a presence. And suddenly she wasn't. In that terrible gravel playground, no less. I remember that damned playground all too well. You all have pebbles embedded in your knees to this day from that damned playground. That poor child.

And to be struck in the one place that she would have thought about a thousand times, said my dad quietly, stirring his tea. People think it is about celibacy but from what I understand of those who give their lives in spiritual service it is much more about loneliness. Imagine as you say yes with immense joy you know you are also saying no forever to the quickening of life in your belly. Imagine knowing that you would never have children of your own but would have to find glints and hints of your own sons and daughters among strange children. Imagine that even the children you were able to love as a teacher or a nurse would never be the children you would see burning toast in the morning or falling asleep in the car on the way home from the beach.

And we did imagine that, the three of us, in silence, at the old ash table, stirring our tea. Outside I remember there was a mockingbird who surely could have had a career in opera had he or she chosen to go in that direction. After a while my mother said We always took them for granted and we still do, don't we? The poor girls. So very much the best of us, weren't they? Aren't they? And my dad said that's absolutely so, that's absolutely so.

V.

THE ROOM IN THE FIREHOUSE

I went to a meeting with a friend yesterday. It was early in the morning in our town's firehouse. The firemen have lent a room to this meeting for thirty years. My friend was rattled and defensive. It was the first time my friend had been to such a meeting. We sat in a quiet corner. Most people sat against the walls but a few sat at a table in the center of the room. There were women and men of all ages. The young man next to me fidgeted the entire ninety minutes of the meeting except when it was his turn to speak. A woman across from us knitted a brilliant red scarf furiously the whole meeting, stopping only when it was her turn to speak. People took turns speaking. There was no particular order. A slight man in a baseball cap spoke first. He was wry and funny about the hash he had made of his life. Most of the people who spoke were wry and funny. One man's voice shook when he spoke and the man next to him reached over and put his gnarled hand on his shoulder. Even though many of the speakers were wry and funny, their stories were not. Their stories were awful. Wives walking out the door with children; and police cars and police vans and police officers and court judges and probation officers, and broken teeth and bones; and having to camp in city parks; and companions who froze to death in alleys; and waking up in strange rooms with strange people; and your own children quietly locking the door when they saw it was you on the front porch; and security officers escorting you off the premises as you walked along with all the stuff that had been in your office cubicle now crammed into a big cardboard box; and walking out of meetings like this because meetings like this were for losers, not for *you*, and *you* didn't need this vaguely religious holding-hands crap; and then sitting by the door so you could leave when it got to be too much, and then later taking a seat all the way inside, and maybe someday you will even sit at the table, although sitting at the table means you have to be savagely honest with yourself and everyone else about what you cannot do without help, and being that kind of desperately honest is unbelievably awfully hard.

But I sat in a quiet corner of the firehouse yesterday and listened as one person after another *was* that searingly honest, *did* speak openly and ruefully about what one man called the delicious disaster, and I was so moved I could not speak for some moments after the meeting ended. My friend was not moved at all and strode out of the meeting glad it was over and dismissive of *those poor people*. I wish my friend was not dismissive of those poor people. It seems to me that those poor people are the wealthiest people I ever saw in honest humility. It seems to me they are battling ferociously to turn horror into some small shivering peace and maybe even someday somehow a shy stagger of joy. It seems to me that they are great because they know they are not, healthy because they know they are ill, admirable because they know they are not admirable at all by all the measures *of the real world,* as another man called the world outside the room of the firehouse.

There was something great in that room. There is something great in all the thousands of rooms like it in America, the millions of rooms like it around the world. I don't have a good word for that great thing, but I saw it, staggering like a new foal, from where I sat silently in the corner. My friend didn't see it, and my friend may never reach for it, and there's nothing I can do to make that happen. Part of the great thing that happens in those rooms, perhaps, is that no one can open that window for anyone else, though everyone can applaud when someone does reach for that crack of light, shyly, shaking a little. I heard that applause several times yesterday morning, in the firehouse, and it sounded like the most wonderful painful music to me.

SWALLOWING AN OTTER

One of the things I loved about my dad in my opening years of being his son was his habit of never snickering at the nutty questions that his many kids asked, and never saying anything at all supercilious, and never issuing any sort of sneering or cutting remark that we remember, although heaven knows the man had endless chances to do so, considering all the careening children he and our mom made over the years, with the "signal & generous assistance of the Principal Engineer," as he said.

This is how he talks to this day, with a wry precision in which you can hear ampersands and initial capital letters, if you listen carefully.

The closest he would come to falling down laughing when you asked him a particularly silly question was to make a sort of gentle chuffing sound deep in his throat, as if he had swallowed an otter and was having a little trouble working it down past his esophagus, and twice I remember asking him something and he made the swallowing-the-otter sound and couldn't stop and had to go lie down for a while until he recovered.

When I was young I assumed that all dads were like my dad and, if you asked them such things as *If a lady does not use her uterus, is it unusederus?*, they would make a sound like they had swallowed most of the otter successfully but its long muscular tail was taking its own sweet time to wriggle down the chute and maybe it was hung up on one tonsil or another which would certainly be a problem, but later in life I learned that actually no dads were like our dad at *all*, and with other dads if you asked them if trees lose their tempers, or why are so many saints grumpy, or do toothbrushes have a mating season, they would say something tart or dismissive rather than make the gentle sound of swallowing an otter.

Our dad made any number of other sounds — he sang once,

suddenly, in church, which many people remember and talk about to this day — and he did all the usual laughing and roaring and humming and crooning and barking expected of dads, but it's that gentle chuffing sound in his throat that comes back to me this morning. He and I were talking about this the other day and I said I wished with all my might that I could remember all the questions I had asked him that made him make that sound, as they seemed like the sort of artlessly nutty questions kids are always asking me now. That sort of utterly open curiosity from children is a lovely and holy thing in the world, such a glorious energy I wish I could collect and channel it toward the darkness, and clean and electrify and hilarify the world, and very faintly in my phone I heard my dad having a bit of trouble swallowing an otter, which is not a sound you hear every day and is absolutely a sound that should be savored and treasured when you are granted the gift of hearing it.

WHAT IS A PRIEST?

Is a question I have asked all of my life since I was about six years old and noticed a brief cheerful Capuchin named Father Hugh at our dinner table every few weeks. He might have been five feet tall on days without humidity and he smoked tremendous cigars and he called our dad Mis Ster Doyle in exactly that cadence which for some reason made both of them grin every time he said it which was often. A priest is a representative of the people, arising from within our midst in answer to the Lord's commanding call, said Sister Marie in school. A priest is first and foremost a servant of the faithful, said Father Paul when he visited our class and shook all our hands with his moist pale hand like a small flounder. A priest is a consecrated witness to and celebrant of the unceasing river of miracles and sacraments, said a Jesuit who visited our parish. Our dad's other best priest friend was Father Norman, who was as big as a cliff or a ship or Brazil where he had once been a missionary. So priests could come in all shapes and sizes and colors from pink to beige to russet to dusk to even apricot like Father Dennis when he was annoyed. A priest is a salesman for the greatest product ever and ideally he is an irresistible advertisement for the Word because of who he *is,* not because of what he says, said Father Norman, booming it out so exuberantly at his end of the table that the good china laid out for the occasion looked nervous. A priest is a sentinel chosen by the Lord to serve as a stalwart bulwark against the subtle armies of Lucifer, said our quietest uncle once, suddenly, to everyone's surprise

A priest is a muddle who does his level best most of the time to be of at least *minimal* service to the Christ in every heart, said Father Hugh, waving his cigar at the mosquitoes on the porch at dusk in summer. If I can be called to the priesthood, clearly any dolt can be a priest. There's no test to pass except the test of every day. It's a profession in every sense of the word. I try to remember to be a testament, as it were. Now, I do that through the written word, as does your estimable father. We are the heirs of Saint Francis de Sales and Teresa of Avila in that sense: storytellers, story-sharers, testifiers, town criers, following in the footsteps of the greatest of storytellers, the finest of Jewish authors, our Lord Jesus. A priest is a man who chooses a life not merely of celibacy but of chastity not only as conscious sacrifice but more importantly as a means to focus all his energies on selfless service to the community of the faithful. A priest is not granted authority by virtue of his vocation but by virtue of his character. A priest is a sort of verb in a suit, said Father Hugh, lighting a second cigar from the awful bedraggled moist remains of the first. He is in a very real sense an apostle in direct descent from the first of us chosen by Himself to carry the message of salvation. You will remember that they too were a motley crew and, no mistake, a collection of bumblers no better than any other twelve stragglers gathered from highways and byways; but they did their best to dimly understand and then boldly disseminate the incredible secret that He had revealed to them first among all men; and ever after our Merciful Lord, ever subtle in His humor, has invited bumblers like me to follow in their halting steps, with no scrip for the journey, nor brass in my purse. So that is what a priest is, my young friend; a shabby traveler on the road, with neither shoes nor stave, speaking the Word as best we can, and bowing low in humble recognition of glowing holiness in others, as for example your glorious and inimitable mother. *When you come into a worthy house, salute it,* says our friend Saint Matthew, first of the four Gospel singers, and *let your peace come upon it,* and so I do salute this house, and all in it, and ask the peace of the Lord upon it, and we had better go back in and help with the dishes, don't you think? What kind of buffoons would we be if we sat here jawing while someone else cleaned the kitchen? *Ora et labora,* as our Benedictine brothers and sisters say!

UNCTION

I'll tell you an anointing story. A priest told it to me. He had been in a war. *The* war, he called it. We didn't think there would ever be another war after *that* war, he said. Too bad we were wrong about that. That would have been a great thing to be right about.

The priest was talking to me as he was walking slowly along the edge of the soccer field named for him at the university where we both worked. He had taught accounting here for many years, but when he got old he just slowly walked around campus talking to students, who loved him. It seemed to me he knew a thousand students by name, but perhaps he didn't know that many. It sure seemed like it, though.

I was a sergeant then, said Father. I wasn't a priest yet. I had thought about being a priest before the war and like a lot of guys I ran screaming away from the idea because I thought it was crazy and it was maybe my mom's idea, not mine, and maybe it meant I wasn't a real man or something like that. *Becoming* a priest is scary. No one admits that. *Being* a priest is scary enough, but you are committed to it after you are ordained, so becoming a priest was scarier, at least to me.

He stopped walking and sat down in a chair by the gate to the soccer field. His chair was always by that gate, rain or shine. One time I asked the field's groundskeeper about Father's chair and he said We make sure there's his chair is there in case he needs to rest. He's not walking as good as he used to, you notice.

I joined the army and went to the war, said Father. I was twenty. They made me a sergeant just to fill out a duty roster. I hadn't done anything to be promoted. My unit ended up in New Guinea. We were with the Australians. Essentially our battle was backing up slowly over a huge mountain range. Fighting backwards. The Japanese pushed us back all day and night. Eventually they were going to push us back into the sea and take over New Guinea and then take over Australia and make it the biggest air base in the history of the world. Well, in the end, we pushed *them* back into the sea, and that was the beginning of the end of their empire. That was the first time they lost a land battle, you know. People forget now. If they didn't lose that battle, who knows?

Soon after Father and I had this conversation about the war he stopped walking altogether and the university gave him a little scooter which he drove slowly everywhere on campus, greeting students by name. You could tell it was him from all the way across the quad because of the scooter and the cheerful white golf cap he wore all the time. One day I noticed that his chair by the soccer field was gone.

But I was telling you an anointing story, said Father. Well, back then it wasn't called anointing. It was extreme unction, and you did it only in times of dire sickness and imminent death. I knew that much from Catholic school and paying attention to our priests. We had *five* priests in our parish. Those were the good old days when there would be a pastor and then a flock of young guys in training to be pastors. I'd seen them anointing old people, and once a girl who had been hit by a truck in our neighborhood, and I paid attention. It was such a gentle sacrament, no fuss and special vestments, and it seemed to me that sometimes it worked just because the sick person believed so intensely that it *would* work, you know?

The day that the university dedicated the soccer field in his name Father was supposed to say a few words, but he couldn't get any words out and he just blinked uncomfortably in the sun for a few seconds and then smiled and waved and sat down. Everyone cheered. His grand-niece said to me later, He would have been a terrific pope except he's just terrible at speaking in public. He's *awful* at speaking in public. He's great speaking in the kitchen or the classroom, but once you get him in front of a crowd oh my god he's terrible. I say that with love. I absolutely love that man.

But unction wasn't primarily about healing, said Father. It was primarily about *spiritual* healing. Getting square with yourself and the Lord before you went home. Remission of sins first and then maybe whatever other healing aspects might happen by intercession. And it was such an *honest* sacrament, you know? The priest would anoint the eyes, ears, nose, mouth, and hands of the sick person, all the doors and windows through which your soul goes out to work in the world; or if things were really dire he would just anoint the head. That happened with the girl who was hit by the truck. He just anointed her head. That was the first time I saw a priest cry. She didn't live another hour. I bet she was all of five years old. She lived two doors down from me on our street and for some reason all the kids on our street were around when the priest anointed her. I remember my brother was outside looking through the window. This was in Chicago.

Finally Father stopped even driving his scooter slowly around campus and there were a couple of months when he didn't come out of his room even for communal meals. He didn't even make it to Mass in the community room because it was in the basement and he couldn't get up and down the stairs and there was no elevator there. Occasionally a few friends would come by his apartment in the priests' quarters and he would celebrate Mass at his kitchen table. One time he baptized the grandson of an alumnus at his kitchen table, using holy oil from a tiny old bottle he kept on his spice rack. I was going to ask him about that bottle but I forgot.

So I was in the battle in New Guinea, said Father, and we were getting hammered, and one night a kid even younger than me got blown up, and me and another guy were the only guys within reach to get to him and be with him as he died. You could tell he was going to die pretty quick. We didn't even call for a medic. He knew too, I think. His eyes were open but he couldn't speak. I saw he had a medal around his neck, the Madonna, and I figured he was Catholic. Some Protestant guys I knew had medals, but never the Madonna. The other guy with me that night was not a religious guy. He was from the state of Washington, I think. Anyway the kid who was dying was staring at me, and for some reason I felt like I should anoint him. I still don't know why. It was something to do. It was the right thing to do, but it wasn't religious, you know what I mean? It was a holy thing. Holy things are bigger than religions, even Catholicism. Religions borrow holy things. That's why a priest sinning is such a terrible thing.

Just before Father was sent back to the home for elderly priests at the headquarters of his order I wrote a brief piece about him for the university's alumni magazine. In that piece he talked at length about how much he loved Oregon, where he had lived and worked for nearly fifty years and how, despite the custom of his order that all of its dead were buried together in a cemetery at headquarters, he would much rather be cremated and scattered in the massive river that burls past the university campus, because he loved the river and had savored it daily for fifty years and it would brush his ashes against the university campus as it went past, which he thought would be sweet and funny. He told me later he got a stern formal letter from his provincial superior about this remark, stating in no uncertain terms that when Father died he would be buried with his fellow priests and brothers in the cemetery at headquarters. He laughed as he told me about this letter. He thought it was funny.

We didn't have any consecrated oil in the jungle, of course, said Father, and we didn't have any consecrated water either, although it was wet as the bottom of the ocean in those mountains, my *God* it was wet. I thought about using a little mud but that didn't feel right, so to be honest with you I used the man's own blood to anoint him before he died. I did. He was bleeding from everywhere. I wiped my hand on my uniform to get it as clean as I could and I took some of his blood and made a cross on his forehead and he looked at me. He knew what I was doing. I start to cry every time I think about that moment, and that was a real long time ago. He knew I was anointing him for death and he closed his eyes for a minute and the other guy with us thought the kid had died but then he opened his eyes and I finished anointing him. I did his eyes and ears and nose and mouth but only one hand because the other was gone. I don't think he even knew it was gone. His legs were a mess also. I don't think he knew how bad he was hurt because he was hurt so bad. But he knew I anointed him. He knew that. He died a couple minutes later. That was the first time I was ever that close to a man when he died and you could actually see the life go out of him. He was alive, and then he just wasn't, and you could tell the instant the soul left his body.

Finally Father was sent to the home for elderly priests at the order's headquarters back east. He returned to Oregon once, when his health appeared to improve some, but then his health slumped again and he was returned to the old priests' home. He was never much for letters but he loved phone calls and one time when I was chatting with him on the phone he told me the only thing that really drove him crazy about being there was the constant inane chatter, as he said, about college football. Let's face facts, he said. It's a militaristic gladiatorial sport, all bombast and naked thirst for violence. All sports are stylized wars, of course, but it seems to me that soccer is much further advanced evolutionarily than football. I tease them here sometimes saying that our soccer team has won a lot more games than their football team. The people here don't like that, no. But it's true.

I tell the story of that kid in the jungle sometimes when I talk to new priests in my order, said Father, and they ask me if that's the reason I became a priest and I say no, no, me becoming a priest was a real long road, a road I started on after the war, but now all these years later I wonder if they were right and I was wrong. That kid needed someone to anoint him and there I was, you know? Someone needed to be there. Being a priest is mostly just being there. You need someone to be there at the very end. Many people maybe have someone they love to be the last person to touch them and say be forgiven, be clean, be peaceful, go with the Lord, but most people don't, you know. Most people are alone. We never admit that. I think that's why we have religions in the end, because we are so alone and religions bring us together at the moments we all know are holy but it's hard to admit it. Sacraments are ways we insist on what's holy. People think sacraments are stiff and boring and formal and just rituals but I don't think so. I try to remember they are ways to insist on holiness, you know what I mean?

The priest who runs the home for old priests told me that Father died at the breakfast table. He was reaching for the jam when he made a pained sound, a sort of surprised grunt you might say, said the priest who runs the home, and his head sank down to the table and that was that. Massive heart attack. Yes, I anointed him, even though I was pretty sure he was gone. Yes, of course I did.

Nowadays we don't call it extreme unction anymore, said Father. Now we say Anointing of the Sick, and there were some men among my priestly brethren who complained and moaned about this, but I could never see that it mattered what you call it. Guys tend to complain about any change at all, of course. There's still a guy I could name who is annoyed that we face the congregation when we celebrate Mass, and that was fifty years ago we turned around, for heaven's sake. Anyway whenever I start getting annoyed at guys complaining I think about that kid in the jungle and he reminds me that we priests are just servants. Our job is to be there when it counts. Any priest who thinks he is cooler or more important or holier than anyone else is an idiot. I try to remember that. I try to remember that at least one time I was there when it counted. Anybody could have done what I did that night, but for some reason it was me. Maybe that was the spark that set me on the road of being a priest. I don't know. It sure was a holy moment, though. I'd like to meet that kid, somehow, after I die, and talk about that moment. I didn't even know the kid, in this life — he had been with us for about three days and no one even really knew his name.

VI.

MASCHINENPISTOLE

And while we are on the subject of summer camps allow me to sing my experience in Boy Scout Camp in the deep forests of the Adirondack Mountains of New York State, long years ago but still fresh to my memory, for not only did we do the usual Scoutish things like build triangular campfires from beech logs and whittle arrows and race rickety canoes but we also stole a camp truck filled with cakes and pies for the other troops' dessert, and slipped out of camp to an amazing nearby diner, and found the rusted shards of what one member of our patrol later ascertained to be a Maschinenpistole used by the Nazi Fallschirmjäger, or paratroopers, in the Second World War.

All these years after we found that scatter of rusted brooding shards of metal in moist shivering ground at the edge of a spruce swamp I wonder how it got from the war over there to the forest here, and who carried it from one haunted wood to another, and why it was smashed to pieces apparently with a ball-peen hammer, and how long it had been moldering there in the swamp, and what had happened to the man or woman or child who smashed it to bits, and who would have eventually discovered it a century or a millennium later, a curious child or an archeology team, and what they would have thought it to be — a shattered religious object, a broken toy, an instrument for some unimaginable music?

If this was a sensible and reasonable essay I would now explain the theft of the dessert truck and how we waylaid the driver, a Star Scout, and borrowed the truck long enough to heroically deliver forty cakes and pies to our camp and then returned the truck to the spot where he had left it when he courageously leapt to the aid of ostensibly injured fellow Scouts; and I would briefly and entertainingly report how we plotted a journey through the moonless swamp to the extraordinary diner where the special was roast turkey with mashed potatoes and gravy; and I might mention odd and riveting moments like the time a boy in my patrol fired a whittled arrow at a hawk and the hawk spun in the air like a dancer and dove on the boy who I believe would have lost an ear had he not himself dove into a tent; but no, I return to the Maschinenpistole, for several reasons.

For one thing several of us discovered it at once, so none could claim ownership or primacy, which was rare; for another we all could tell, just staring at it, that it reeked of death in a cold metallic way that only human beings would inflict on a throbbing green world. And the way we crouched over it together, fascinated and frightened, as we all are by anything evil; and how we stayed there long, unable to joke about it, but unable also to easily walk away and leave it as a grim shrine or to bury it for good and return it to the earth from which it had been forged by men who so wanted a world of gaunt slaves.

If this was fiction or a poem there might be a passage here where we Scouts walked away silently, each boy thinking about the crime of war, the disease of it, the weird way wars are made of courage and grace and rape and insanity all at once; perhaps it would also be dusk, the darkness sifting into the story on little metaphorical feet; but this is a true tale, and we each walked away thinking that we would come back before camp ended and take a piece of the gun as a souvenir and not tell the other guys; but none of us did that, as I discovered years later. Last year I met all those boys again, now large men, at the wedding of one of our sons, and at the reception we talked hesitantly about the Maschinenpistole, and one by one we admitted that we were still rattled by it and remembered the feeling of discovering, a few inches from your face, an evil thing, a thing designed brilliantly and specifically for killing men. As the father of the groom said, *all our genius, and this is what we do with it?*

THE THIRD PERSON

It was the use of the third person that confused me utterly in third grade when we began to discuss The Trinity. We understood, if vaguely, the First Person, the original idea, the progenitor, the instigator of all things, that which spake from the burning bush; we understood, less vaguely because of constant repetition, the Second Person, *that nice Jewish boy,* as my mother liked to say, savoring the dangerous levity; but we were flummoxed and discombobulated by the Third Person, who was (a) not a person and (b) not actually a Ghost, and (c) even more confusing because the lesson just before The Holy Trinity had been grammar, in which we grappled for the first time, not successfully, with the idea of the third person in *discourse, conversation, and rhetorical convention,* said Sister Margaret.

Even at age eight I prided myself on being in the upper seventy percent of the class academically, but of the Third Person who was not a person after a lesson in the third person I could make neither head nor tail. I was not alone in this — even that simpering preening sycophant Maureen M. was stymied, I could tell, because she wasn't for once waving her hand like a thrashing surf rod on a stormy day when the striped bass were running or actually jumping up and down excitedly in her seat so that her desk shimmied out of her row every day or making that idiotic *choose me Sister!* face that we used to try to imitate at home until our mothers caught us and lectured us about ending up Looking like that poor trout-faced Ed Sullivan on television God Help Us All if you continue to grimace like that I will inform your father forthwith.

Sister Margaret, who was the daughter of immigrants from Mayo God Help Us, as she always said, tried the usual shamrock explanation, which led us to believe the Trinity had something to do with agriculture. We still had one last small farm in our town then, and as we processed the idea that the Trinity was not unlike a sprig of clover, three that is at once one, we turned and stared at the son of the farmer, who was a mound of a child afflicted by exploding pens, and concluded privately that if the Holy Trinity had anything whatsoever to do with kids like Anthony M., the Church as a going concern was doomed.

Sister Margaret, no slouch, sensed our confusion and tacked back toward grammar, giving a memorable disquisition about the third person that used our pastor as the example. Our pastor was universally referred to as The Monsignor, period, and the way the words were pronounced you could indeed hear the initial capital letter on the word The; occasionally strangers or new people to the parish would call him Father, or Father Stephen, or Monsignor His Last Name, but The Monsignor had a glacial stare and an alpine dignity that soon set things aright. Now, The Monsignor himself, said Sister Margaret, when referring to himself, uses the first person singular; when speaking to someone else, or being spoken to, he uses, or hears, the second person singular; but when he is being referred to indirectly, we use the third person for him and call him The Monsignor, isn't that so? But in all three cases he remains himself, even though he is the first, second, and third person. You see? One that is also three, three that is at once one. Any questions?

Thus it was that I spent a fair piece of my childhood thinking of The Monsignor as the Holy Spirit, and I can safely say that this elucidated a great deal about the glorious mystery of that immensely subtle and brilliant aspect of Catholic theology, for The Monsignor was a deft and subtle being, able to influence everyone without seeming to make any effort, able to inspire better and more creative performance without hector and thunder, claiming no credit for and leaving no trace of his stimulating presence, infusing all things with his spirit but assuming nothing like a form that we could understand as human. He was a steady and enduring energy, accessible to anyone at any time by all accounts, and inexhaustible; he had the great skill of affirming what you wanted to do, which meant you did it briskly and happily because it was your idea or you thought it was; he had the gift of silence, which not only can be wonderfully eloquent but richly productive of eloquence and articulation; and he refused to be photographed, even at functions at which he was presiding spirit, so that there is no evidence of his astonishing beneficial effect but only a vague feeling among those who had been inspired that something slightly more than their usual selves was at work or at least something had been of silent but powerful assistance in luring or welcoming their best selves from the usual muddle.

In later years, of course, what with higher Catholic education, my brilliant and subtle parents, and many piercingly wise companions along the road, I learned that The Monsignor was probably not, in himself, as a man named Stephen, *in se ut homo,* the Holy Spirit, the Third Person of the Holy Trinity; but I continue to think, all these years later, that you could do a lot worse than use him for an example when trying to explain something which cannot be explained except by telling a story. It turns out that there are lots of things you cannot explain except by telling stories, which do not explain or define or account them hardly at all but do give us a subtle and telling sense of what it is we mean when we use words like *holy* and *miracle* and *God.*

TIDE TABLE

Very rarely are we able to reach back into the past and mark a moment where our innermost tides began to flow in another direction; but I think I see one, a moment when I realized with a first hint of cold honesty I was being a selfish buffoon and possibly the moment where I began to grow up.

It is beside the point that it took me another ten years at least to get there, or that I am not quite there yet, even in my fifties.

I was sitting at the dining-room table. My dad and my mom and my sister were sitting there also. I believe it was lunch. My brothers were elsewhere committing misdemeanor. I believe it was summertime. The room was lined with books from floor to ceiling. I believe the meal was finished and my mother and sister were having tea and cigarettes. My father mentioned casually that our cousins were coming for dinner or next Sunday or something like that. I believe these were the Connecticut cousins and not the New York cousins.

I shoved my chair back and whined and snarled and complained. I believe this had something to do with some vague plans of my own that I had of course not shared with anyone else as yet, probably because they were half-hatched or mostly imaginary.

My father said something calm and reasonable, as still is his wont. I said something rude. My mother remonstrated quietly but sharply, as still is her wont. I said something breathtakingly selfish. My sister said something gentle and kind, as still is her wont. I said something cutting and sneering and angry. My mother slowly put down her tea. Odd that I would remember that detail, her cigarette in her left hand and her teacup in her right and the cup descending slowly to the table. The table had a quiet blue cloth, and just outside the window the yew hedge was the most brilliant vibrant green.

As I remember it was just as my mother was putting her teacup on the table, just as the smoke from the cigarettes was rising thin and blue and unbroken like twin towers, just as my father put his big hands on the table and prepared to stand up and say something calm and blunt to me and cut the moment before it spun out of control, that I realized I was being a fool.

It wasn't an epiphany or a trumpet blast or anything epic. It was an almost infinitesimal wriggle of something for which I don't have good words even now. It wasn't that I was embarrassed, though I was embarrassed later. It was more like for a second I saw who I actually was rather than who I thought I was, or wanted to be, or wanted other people to think I was. I understood, dimly, for an instant, I believe for the first time in my life, that I was being a fool.

I kept right on being a fool, of course. You cannot escape yourself that quickly, not as a teenager, or later either, it turns out. Often you keep playing a bad hand even when you know it's a terrible hand and you should laugh and throw down your cards and say something self-deprecating and apologize and tiptoe into the next moment. Often you stay inside the prison of your confidence and ostensible dignity even as you peer through the bars, embarrassed.

As I remember I stormed off and the world spun on relentlessly through the stars and the cousins came over and we all grew much older and eventually the house was sold and God alone knows where that dining-room table is. It might still be in the house, and it might still be covered with a blue cloth, and there might even now even this very moment be a seething teenager sitting at it, facing the yew hedge, seeing a hint of who he might grow up to be if he can stop being a fool. With all my heart, with all my heart, I wish him well.

MPILO

A while ago I was in a room with a small older man and a number of college students. The room was small and the students were many. The older man was the color of copper. The students were all different colors from rose to smoke to midnight. There were so many students that some sat on the floor and on windowsills and on a desk behind the older man. The older man had been a bishop in a country far away and he spoke with a swing and rhythm in his cadence that took a while to get used to. Also he laughed a lot, so between his giggling and his lilt it took us a few minutes to catch his music clearly, but after that we were all on the same page.

He answered questions. There were a lot of questions. Many were about life in Africa and the quiet revolution he had fomented and seen happen almost miraculously, but some were about the revolutions he still fomented — emotional and spiritual revolutions, more than political ones, as he said, laughing. He said really his whole life was one long revolution. He said his whole life as a man of the cloth had begun when he was twelve years old and walking down the street with his mother and a priest stopped and took off his hat to his mother, a gesture of respect in every culture on earth, which means, *here is my head, take it if you want,* he said, laughing. He said this kind act made him very interested in the priest's tribe. What sort of tribe was *this* that respected people of all colors? And so he became a priest, but not the sort of priest we had here at our college, who could not get married, he said; he became the sort of priest who could get married, and that was *fun!*

He laughed and we all laughed but then a student raised her hand and very quietly asked him this question: What is the point of evolution?

He stopped laughing and looked closely to see who had asked this question, and then he walked as close as he could get to her in the press of bodies and he said, Sister, that is a good question. I have thought a great deal about that question. I do not know the answer. But I will tell you a story.

With my own eyes I have seen murderers kneel down and beg forgiveness from the mothers and fathers of children they murdered, and I have seen mothers step forward and reach down and cup the faces of the murderers in their hands and say *I forgive you.* I saw this happen not once but many times. I saw this with my own eyes and no one can gainsay me. I saw children forgive the slaying of their parents, sisters the slaying of their brothers, wives the slaying of their husbands. *I saw this happen.* I do not know how it can happen. I cannot make sense of such grace and mercy. It doesn't *make* sense. Maybe that is the secret. We hunger and rage for justice but there is something past justice that can happen and sometimes it *does* happen. I have seen it with my own eyes. I do not know if I would be large enough in heart to forgive such things, and me a man of the cloth, who swore his life to the idea! But I am small and forgiveness is vast. I have seen these things with my own eyes and I cannot forget what I saw. That is my answer to your question. What is the point of human beings? *That* is the point. I think we are here to get to there. That is what I think. I could be wrong. So many times I have been wrong! But I do not think I am wrong about this. No.

A few minutes later Mpilo Desmond Tutu, Archbishop Emeritus of the Anglican Church of Southern Africa, whose name means hope in his native language, was hustled off by his handlers to give a cheerful headlong laughing piercing talk before a crowd of thousands, but before he left he bowed to the students and said *Pray for me, I need it!,* and everyone laughed. A few minutes later the room was empty, but I have never been able to forget what he said, and now I hope you never forget either. Maybe we will get there sooner than later if we remember those words.

LITTLE KIDS IN MASS

The daily noon Mass on campus is sparsely attended, to be polite, on the best days, but on days when the students are on break the attendance can be skeletal. But not today. Today, to my amazement, there are four-year-old twin boys in front of me, complete with their parents, the father immensely tall and the mother adamantly not.

The noon Mass is legendary for starting on the button and never going more than 25 minutes, because afternoon classes start at 12:30 and you want to give students a chance to sprint in their flip-flops to class after Mass, and for the first five minutes the twins sit quietly and respectfully and perhaps even reverently, each in his seat between mom and dad. This does not last. At 12:07 I see the first flurry of hands and elbows as they jockey and joust. At 12:11 one of them amazingly pulls a bunch of grapes from his pocket and begins to eat some and lose the rest. At 12:13 there are easily a dozen grapes and both boys under the chairs. At 12:15 the mom, clearly a veteran of these sorts of things, pulls two cookies from her pockets for the boys. At 12:20 the dad finally bends down from his great height and tersely reads his sons the riot act, a moment I have been waiting for with high collegial glee, for I have been in his shoes: I have been in Mass in this very chapel with my small twin sons, who have dropped Cheerios from the balcony onto the bald spots of congregants below and stuck their arms in the baptistry just to see what it would feel like and made barnyard noises at exactly the wrong moments and ran all around the chapel shaking hands stickily with startled bemused congregants at the Sign of Peace.

After Mass I say to the priest with a smile that it is not every day we are graced by rambunctious ruffians who scatter grapes and crumbs on the floor and giggle and yawn and shimmy and snicker and lose their shoes and drop hymnals on the floor with a terrific bang and pay no attention whatsoever to the Gospel readings and the homily and the miracle of the Eucharist but rather gaze raptly at the life-size cedar crucifix and try to blow out a candle on the altar as their parents carry them up for a blessing and say *hi!* to the grinning priest as he lays his hand upon their innocent brows and spend the last five minutes of Mass sitting in the same seat trying to shove the other guy off but only using your butt and not your hands; and the priest, unforgettably, says this to me: I love little kids in Mass. I love it when they misbehave. I love it when they are bored and pay no attention and squirm. I love it when they get distracted by a moth and spend five minutes following the moth's precarious voyage among the lights. It's all good. They are being soaked in the Mass. They hear the words and feel the reverence and maybe they even sense the food of the experience, you know? Sometimes people complain and make veiled remarks about behavior and discipline and parental control and decorum and the rapid dissolution of morals today and stuff like that, and I have no patience for it. For one thing *they* were little kids in Mass once, and for another if there are no little kids in Mass, pretty soon there won't be any Masses. You have to let kids be kids. I love little kids in Mass. If you are distracted by a little kid being a little kid you are not focused on what's holy. Little kids are holy. Let it be. My only rule is no fistfights. Other than that I don't care about grapes and yawning. I think the cadence and the rhythm and the custom and the peace of the Mass soaks into kids without them knowing it. That's why a lot of the students here come back to Mass, I think — it sparks some emotional memory in them; and once they are back in Mass here, then they pay attention in new ways and find new food in it. It's all good. The more the merrier. I don't mind dogs when I celebrate Mass, either. For one thing they are generally better behaved than little kids, but for another I figure the Mass soaks into them too and how could that be bad? You know what I mean?

I say I do know very well what he means and we shake hands and he heads to the sacristy to disrobe and I head back to work, but about halfway back to my office I feel awfully sad that I do not have grapes and cookies in my jacket pockets. I don't even have shards of ancient Cheerios anymore, and there were years there when my pockets were so filled with brittle crumbs that birds followed me in rotation, sparrows in the morning and crows in the afternoon. For a minute I want to shuffle back to the chapel and catch that tiny mom and ask her for a cookie, just because, but then I realize that she will think I am a nut. I had my run as the dad of little kids squirming in Mass. It was a sweet glorious unforgettable run, too, and now it's someone else's turn, and how good and holy that is, that there are still little kids under the seats, paying no attention whatsoever.

But they will.

THE ANSWER IS
IN THE QUESTIONING

That was the very last thing my brother Kevin said before he died. He died on the first day of summer two years ago. Six words, after millions of words spoken and read and taught and typed over sixty years. He had been a college professor.

We give great weight to last words, the words spoken on the precipice. Most of the time I would guess that those words are about love. I would guess that many of those words have something to do with light. I would guess that some of those final words are shrieks or gasps or utterances of astonishment.

The answer is in the questioning.

I have thought about those six words for two years now, since I first heard them. It turns out you can ponder them from every conceivable angle and never get to the bottom of what they mean. He spoke them with authority, says his wife, who was there. He spoke them with a sort of amazement, as if he had finally realized something crucial, says his friend the deacon, who was there. Did he mean that if you ask a question, the answer is inside it somewhere? Did he mean that everything we have always been desperate to know is alive inside our curiosity? Was he talking about what we mean when we use the word *God?*

My brother was not a man to use words lightly. He was not much for small talk. He was not much for airy remarks or banter. If you asked him a question he would be silent for a moment, thinking, and then silent for another moment, composing his answer, and then he would answer, succinctly. In his early years he could be curt and terse and tart and rude, but in his later years he was never any of those things that I remember. One of the things I loved about him was that if he did not know the answer to a question he would say (after pondering for a moment) *I do not know,* four lovely words when ordered in that fashion. Many of us issue answers with unwarranted confidence, sometimes when we know full well we do not know a hint or shred of the answer. Or we speak before we think, or issue opinion rather than answer, or issue someone *else's* opinion, or issue opinions so ossified by years of neglect that you could stand them in the corner with the umbrellas and the walking sticks.

The answer is in the questioning.

Did he mean we are verbs and not nouns? Did he mean that as long as we quest we are answered? Did he mean that curiosity, the itch to know, the urge to inquire, the eager opening of doors and windows each to each, the desire to know a new intricacy of the maze or another level of the mystery or another revelation of the relentless miracle is the answer to every question, is why we are here? Could it be that every answer we yearn for is answered already? Could that be what we mean when we talk about God?

Kevin died in his house on a little hill. His house was once the only house for miles around, when it was a farmhouse. From his window he could see a sugar maple and a fir tree and crows and a tatter of the smiling sky. He spoke his last six words in the morning and he died in the afternoon. *The answer is in the questioning.* He had been a brilliant mathematician and he told me once that mathematics was a sort of language and literature and music all at once. You could almost *sing* it, sometimes, he said. He died around four in the afternoon, just about the time the sun would have swung in the window to his left. For many thousands of years the sun is what we meant when we spoke of God. The sun was the answer to all questions. Perhaps the last thing my brother felt in this world was the sun on his face. Light is a language too, when you think about it. You can ask questions in it and the answers always seem to be yes.

VII.

MARGARET

I was good and she was better. Her name was Margaret. She was first and I was second. Her hair was so amazingly red that old ladies at Mass wanted to touch it. She was best and I was not. She had an ocean of freckles on her face and neck and arms and legs. She earned gold stars and I earned silver stars. I wore spectacles and fought anyone who made fun of my spectacles. She was mostly quiet and studious but sometimes she would issue a small cry of triumph when her test paper came back with gold stars and exclamation points. Maybe no one else heard that sound but I did. She was neat and had perfect handwriting. I crammed papers in my pockets and drew all over my notebooks, and pens were always exploding in my shirt pockets. She was cool to me but I was cold to her. I yearned to be the best student in the class just *once*. I yearned for the day Sister Marie would hand our papers back and with an expression of surprise which she could not conceal she would hand me *my* paper first and there would be gold stars and exclamation points! on *my* paper and then she would hand Margaret her paper with silver stars and make a small joke about ice forming over the roiling seas of hell.

I do not know why this was so important to me. I have no idea why. I was a happy boy with parents and brothers and a sister and no one beat me and there were no starving holes in my soul where love should have been and wasn't. Why did I care so about being the best?

The fact is we hardly know anything about ourselves even after years of thinking about ourselves. I had no sense of perspective. I had no sense of proportion. It was only sixth grade. What difference does it make who is the best in the class and who is second when you are twelve years old? But it made a difference to me. I wish now it had not made a difference. Maybe I was frightened of not being as cool and smart and charming as my brothers and sister. Maybe Margaret was frightened of not being the best, too. Maybe *she* had to be the best because of a hole in her soul where love should have been. I never knew and never bothered to ask. It was easier to be annoyed and peevish and finally cruel. This was in April. It was a brilliant day. We were on the playground. I was in a knot of boys and I wanted to be cool and I said that Margaret's face looked like a dog had eaten red peppers and thrown up on her. I said there were more freckles on her face than there were places without freckles. I said she must have been born in the freckle factory and got them for free and took all she could take. I said that God forbid she ever got a tan because then she would be one huge freckle. I said if she marries a man with freckles there will be an epidemic. I *said* these things. I vomited them out one after another quick and easy and casual and the boys laughed and two boys ran to regale the other kids with my hilarious remarks and the snide and sneer of my words went rocketing and thrashing around the playground quick as can be. Some kids laughed and other kids just turned to look at me silently. When the bell rang we got on our wavering motley lines to go back to class and I heard jeering and laughing but I was busy punching a friend and did not catch the details and object of the jeering. As we filed into class I saw three girls huddled at the dim end of the hallway. Two girls were bending and comforting one girl between them the way girls and women do, with hands and murmurs.

The girl in the middle was Margaret and she was sobbing so hard she was gasping, but she wasn't making any noise which was more frightening than if she had been screaming. I hesitated at the door to the classroom and then the boy behind me gave me a shove and I stumbled in and sat in my seat and knew in my soul that I had done a truly evil thing. I have never forgotten that feeling. I have tried to forget. Believe me I have tried. But I cannot forget. Maybe I cannot forget because it was the first time I knew for a cold fact that I had done an evil thing and that I was fully and easily capable of evil and that all the rest of my life would be a struggle against the evil that wriggled inside me, ready to slip out quick as can be.

Maybe that was the first time I was truly deeply honestly ashamed of myself. I was twelve. Somehow some part of me will always be twelve and sitting in the last seat of the first row of desks. Maybe that's a good thing. Maybe that's what we mean when we use the word conscience. We use that word so easily and casually but it is a ferocious and terrifying thing and it is not easy or casual. I never apologized to Margaret. I wish I had. Maybe I will now. I think this is the time and place, finally.

Wherever you are now, Margaret, I ask you to forgive me.

THE LITTLE THINGS
THAT ARE NOT LITTLE

I know what you think of when I say the words *University of Notre Dame du Lac.* You think of the dome, first and foremost, gleaming in the distance like the glowing business end of a stupendous baby bottle, and then you think of your shaggy and peculiar roommates, which makes you snicker; and then you think of vast and epic snow-falls, and of football Saturdays, and of certain people you kissed that we need not talk about here, and about that one almost-romance that you still think about sometimes but don't tell anyone about, there being no need, but you will always wonder a little what if? Then maybe you think about the echoing tumult of voices in the dining hall at lunchtime, or sprawling on the quad, or that unbelievable road trip oh my gawd what were we thinking, and then maybe you think about a teacher who really made you snap awake and think about the subject at hand as more than a means to a grade; and then maybe you think about how great and awful graduation was, and how incredibly boring the speaker was, and how one of your friends wore nothing but his Spiderman underpants under his gown, and isn't it amazing that such a doofus could be a partner in a law firm today? Wouldn't it be funny to mail Spiderman underpants to all the partners in his firm, anonymously, just for kicks?

But it's the next layers of things to think about that interest me this morning. The ranks of tall grasses by the lake, arranged in height order by mysterious natural command. The hollow rattle of basket-balls in the Rock, like a staccato code that no one has ever cracked. The seethe of wind in the trees near Walsh and Sorin, an oratorio never sung the same way twice. The ancient musty scholarly smell of old hall attics where many a frightened freshman has huddled, and stared out the tiny windows, and wondered why why why did I come here so far from home, so competitive, so lonely, why? The wriggles of smoke twisting and swirling from a hundred grills on Saturday mornings, like the ephemeral rigging of invisible airships. The creak of transoms over doors in the oldest halls and the smooth silent metallic rush of elevators in the new; the motley platoons of bicycles, free and easy when loose but camped together in dense packs when buckled in for the night, all shouldered together as if each needed to touch the others to be sure they are near; the day when everyone wears shorts and sandals suddenly as if a memorandum was circulated secretly at dawn that Today We Retire Pants and Shoes; the prevalence of cassocks on certain days and even occasionally, rarest of birds, a bishop in full ornamental magenta, burnished and bright against bricks and maples.

The little things that are not little. The exuberance of sparrows near Lafortune, the boldest of which have organized gangs of their fellows to extort cookies from shyer students. The tiny alleys and walkways and corners and corridors all over campus that take you a year at least to find and milk for solitude and sunlight. The thump of bees against chapel windows. The skreeeek of chairs in a classroom, the confident hum of descending screens, the clatter of keyboards, the muffled ringing of a phone in a purse in the pocket of a jacket in the back of the room and the next instant in which everyone in the room thinks it is his phone or her phone and the next instant when almost everyone realizes wait a minute that's not my phone and the next instant when you grin at the slight discomfiture of the owner of the phone. The subtle architectural and artistic details on campus that take three years to even notice let alone savor, and just when you realize there are a hundred more you have not seen it is time to graduate and move away and begin your wild and lovely life, during which you occasionally pause, struck by an angle of light, or the brush of cedar against stone, or the sheen of a lake, or the thrill of bells, or the flicker of a cassock across a sprawl of grass, and remember when you were young, long ago and far away, at the

University of Notre Dame du Lac; and you are still there, somehow, sometimes; like now.

FATHER JIM

One day not long ago I was walking across the campus where I work when a slender smiling older priest walked past and said *good morning,* and I nearly fainted for he was, no kidding, the Congregation of Holy Cross priest who had taught me freshman geology forty years before at another university far away in snow country, and here he inarguably was, looking exactly the same except for silver in his hair, and so it was that I discovered that Father Jim had retired from teaching and returned home to his native waters, not unlike the salmon and steelhead for which he used to fish as a boy in the cold wild rivers of the Oregon coast.

He told me about his boyhood on a fruit farm atop a small mountain west of the city; his father grew apples and peaches and cherries and pears and walnuts, and his grandparents, who lived downhill, grew wine grapes; his grandfather would tap the barrels every day at noon, ostensibly to test the wine, but not really, says Father Jim, smiling.

We hunted raccoons and fished as much as we could, he says, because we were so high up there was a good deal of snow, more than the valley ever gets, and sometimes my dad would have to leave the car down below and we would all walk up through the snow to the farm. My brother and I went to Saint Cecelia's for grade school and the bus would drop us off at the bottom of the mountain and we would climb up about a mile. It never occurred to me that walking was work, no.

I didn't have any ideas about becoming a priest until I was deep into my twenties, says Father Jim, smiling. By then I was almost finished with my doctorate in geology. I remember it was a Franciscan monk who asked me if I had ever considered being a priest. I answered honestly that it had occurred to me, but not as a hunger of any sort, and he said *well, you ought to try it out,* and this somehow made sense to me, so I did. I vividly remember the one moment when I hesitated; I was in the seminary, deep in snow country, and I woke up one morning and stared at myself in the mirror and thought *I don't want to be here.* There was a long pause and then I started laughing, because I realized I had never had that thought before, in two years of seminary, much of it deep silence; and that was that, for hesitation.

I taught geology for many years, says Father Jim, and now I am retired, and happily so, although I still think of all the students who did not pass my classes and I feel badly about them. Perhaps I could have been a better teacher for them. I do not, for example, remember you in my classes, because you passed, and I do not remember the good and mediocre students, but I remember every one of those who were not so good. Perhaps I could have helped them more than I did. Perhaps that is what I did not do very well as a priest and will have to discuss with the Father when my time comes.

My brother still lives on the mountain, says Father Jim. He grows trees. Our farm was sold and divided up for houses. I don't mind. The soil wasn't very good for farming, to be honest. It's only good for grapes, because it's thin and rocky soil and because of the sharp pitch of the slope. There are three vineyards up there now, which is good use of the land. I go up there sometimes to see my brother. I walk through some of the same trees that were there when I was a boy. There is a thicket of memories there, you could say. The last time I was on the mountain I stopped at one of the vineyards and had a glass of wine and thought about my grandfather. Then I walked up to the top of the mountain, now a nature preserve. It was a lovely day and it seemed to me you could see for eighty miles and eighty years in every direction.

CATCH

One time when I was young, a thousand years ago, I decided to play baseball for the Catholic league team, even though I was terrified of the tiny rocky ball and did not at all understand the supposedly pastoral allure of the sport, which seemed painfully slow and jerky to me, and rather selfish to boot; as far as I could tell the pitcher surrendered the ball only with the greatest reluctance, after pondering the matter grimly for a long time and shaking his head at the catcher; and then when he did finally take leave of the ball he did so with unseemly petulance, flinging it angrily at the batter or the catcher or the umpire, hitting one or another of these poor unfortunates at every turn. Meanwhile the fielders adjusted their private parts, or shouted fervid nonsensical things, or spat copiously into the copious dust, or pounded their mitts angrily, as if their poor cowhide mitts had done anything but idly gape as the pitcher simmered on the mound and the fielders scratched their private parts and the umpire made loud inarticulate hooting sounds when the ball hit the backstop or the batter or the catcher or even the umpire, who hid behind the catcher to provide a smaller target for the furious pitcher.

All in all the game seemed peculiar to me, but several of my friends suddenly had decided to play, so I did so too, of course, even though I had never played before. My father, who was and is a wry soul, pointed out to me that being generally unsure of baseball's regulations and what he called the rhythm and geometry of the game were substantive drawbacks, and he offered to have a catch so that I could understand the basic transaction of the sport, as he said, which is the exchange of the ball; everyone talks about *hitting*, he said, but hitters do not actually hit much or effectively, and even when they do manage to interrupt the ball before it hits the backstop or the umpire, often it goes awry, which is called a fouled or vulgar ball, or it is hit directly at the fielders, who are expected to defend themselves;

so that learning to snare and share the ball is crucial, just as in your beloved basketball, although in baseball the actual ball is tiny and granitic, because the game is descended from cricket, which also has a tiny hard ball, probably because the English are a parsimonious and masochistic race and actually enjoy affliction, which is a sin and one reason their savage empire collapsed.

This was and is how my dad talks, which has provided an endless source of education and entertainment over the years; it was a great shock for us to discover, in late childhood, that other dads did not talk this way, with this bemused sidelong imaginative twist, so that you would be educated and entertained and epiphanated, as my sister once said, all at once, on any subject whatsoever, from empires to umpires and back again.

So out we went in the street for a catch. This is a remarkable sentence for any number of reasons: my dad and I had never had a catch, neither of us had ever held or thrown a baseball before, and neither of us had ever worn cattle-skin hand guards. The whole thing was so amazing that all my brothers came out in the street also, to see this incredible moment; and this flood of brothers was savory bait for the rest of the kids on the block, of which there were many, so very soon there were dozens of children in the street, gaping at the sight of *Mister Doyle!* with a baseball glove on his left hand and a baseball held jauntily in his right.

I should pause here to explain again how unthinkable this was at that time on that street. The other dads in the street would occasionally pop off their porches and trot heavily into the street and toss baseballs and footballs, wearing ragged sweatshirts and Old Man Pants and second-best shoes, but our dad had never set foot in the middle of the street between the tight rows of cars, and the very idea of him jumping off the porch and trotting into the street was beyond the reach of human imagination. Our dad was a tall burly dignified man of fifty who wore a fedora hat and an excellent topcoat when he strode briskly to the train along the sidewalk every morning on his way into the city to work as a journalist. He was erudite and witty and literary. He had read everything and wrote for magazines and was avuncular and wise and the kind of dad you turned to for quiet advice, the kind of dad whose most terrifying remark to his children was *Could I have a word with you?* He was not at all the kind of dad who leapt off the porch and trotted out into the street wearing a ragged sweatshirt. I think if we had ever seen him emerge from the house in a ragged sweatshirt our heads would have exploded right there by the azalea bushes and Mom would have been annoyed.

This is not to say that our dad was unathletic, or unfamiliar with brawn and sport and violence; he had been a college tennis player, and then a sergeant and then lieutenant in the United States Army in not one but two wars, and he had at least once used his fists in anger, that we knew of, and he was well over six feet tall, and in the rare moments he was furious he had a grim glare that could peel paint. But those moments were rare, in our experience; indeed so rare that they had become faint legend, things that had happened long ago and now were imperfectly remembered.

But that one spring afternoon he did step into the street, wearing a baseball glove he had found somewhere, and he did rear back and throw a baseball to me, and this is still, forty years later, a stunning thing to contemplate, for I can still see him, as clear as if it was yesterday, standing tall and relaxed in the street, with his shirt sleeves rolled up and his burly arm cocked to throw me the ball and dozens of children standing on the curbs, crowding as close as they could get to the street without actually being in it to see, no kidding, *Mister Doyle!* throwing a baseball to *Brian*. It was a wonder that no enterprising child sold tickets to the event, which I would not have put past the children at the northwest end of the street, two of whom are now guests of the City of New York.

My memory is imperfect now, so I cannot remember the number of successful exchanges of the tiny and granitic ball, signed by Ed Kranepool of the New York Mets; I believe it passed between us three or four times; let us say three, a holy number, the number of aspects of God in the ancient religious tradition of our family; but on the fourth attempt, as the ball left my father's hand, I lost track of it, being a boy with dense spectacles and perhaps awed by the weight of the unthinkable moment and the murmuring crowd, and the ball hit me, at what I remember as terrific velocity, in the right eye, and down I went.

Sometimes when my brothers and I tell this story now we concentrate on my subsequent incredible black eye (something of a misnomer, for blue and green and yellow were also involved), or the miraculous fact that shards of glass did not pierce my eye and turn me into a larval cyclopean essayist, or the way that our dad went from a standing start thirty feet away to my side in about an eighth of a second, or how that early mishap proved all too predictive of my later misadventures in baseball, in which I ended up being a pitcher who hit the backstop or the batter or the umpire more than the catcher; but I have always preferred to celebrate the moment before the mishap, not the mishap itself. Mishaps are normal, but extraordinary moments are quiet miracles, I think, especially when accompanied by many children pouring out of their houses and crowding together along the curb to witness something they had never seen before and would never see again. A moment like that ought to be resurrected and celebrated regularly, sung for the gift it is; and when I do so, I have discovered, time dissolves, and the past is present, and my dad is fifty again and tall and bemused in the middle of the street between the tight rows of cars, and he rears back to whip the ball to me, and it's always hanging there, fresh from his hand, stunning.

I REMEMBER, I REMEMBER

All the children in my large family went to Catholic grade school named for a French priest who heard confessions sometimes twenty hours a day, which is why he went to heaven even though he was French, as our mother liked to say, her face sharp behind the tendrils of steam from her cup of tea. Our mother was Irish and was still annoyed at the French for not coming to the aid of the Irish against the imperial slavemaster English in 1798, the summer war for independence, *Éirí Amach na nÉireannach Aontaithe,* from May to September, which might well have freed us a century earlier, if only the French had managed to land their ships. How hard is it to land ships and fight for your friends against their slavemasters?, she said, glaring at our dad, who was about to say, yet again, Now, darling, that was long ago and far away and we are all Americans, but our mother had what she called the long memory; *is cuimhim liom,* she would say, I remember, I remember.

It was a wonder to us then and after that she remembered things that had happened long before she was born and remembered them clear and detailed as the Gospels; the Hunger, by which the English blithely allowed a million Irish to starve and so cleared the land of its obstreperous natives so that the gentry would have more room for horses and adultery and the murder of innocent foxes; the penal laws, by which the English ingeniously forbade the natives their language, their religion, education, the ownership of homes and property, the right to defend their homes and families from attack and theft, and even the right to shelter and adopt the orphaned children of their own brothers and sisters and cousins. If you had set out to decimate a people and a culture as thoroughly and meticulously as possible, she would say, if you had moved heaven and earth to find the best means of erasing a culture, you could not *possibly* come up with a better and more efficient system than the English applied to the Irish over the course of four centuries since the day Cromwell, may he burn forever in the cellar of hell, stabled his horses in our churches; the foul evil cur, may he beg for forgiveness until the day of judgment, and may it never be granted him by the infinite grace of God.

The long memory was indeed long, and was never extinguished in the least whatsoever and alternately delighted and terrified her children, who were entertained at the eloquent vituperation she heaped upon the English, much ballyhooed for the elevated attitude of their empire, she would say, which is supposed to have generally raised the level of education in its colonies and brought cricket and soccer to every end of the earth and exported at least the rudiments of democracy to many peoples familiar only with an ancient despotism; but I count millions of murders, and incalculable theft, and an arrogance of spirit bigger than the sprawl of their cursed imperial corporation, on which the sun never set, until it all rightfully dissolved, by clash of arms or a wonderful patience on the part of the enslaved. It was all for money and none other reason, whatever the perfumed lie issuing from their articulate tongues; and ever thus empires, which are vast factories to turn the bodies of slaves into the jingle of coins.

You stare at me with your solicitous smiles, our mother would sometimes say quietly, from behind the wriggling tendrils of steam from her tea, and you say that the past is past and no concern of ours, but look ye to our own nation and its urge to empire and beware the maimed and dead who are the price of imperial commerce; and remember that while it is a virtue and miracle to forgive, it is a damnable sin to forget, and I remember those who withered and wept under the lash in the years gone by. I pray for you that you also keep in mind what ought not to be forgotten and never think the past is dead but remember that the present is pregnant with it and those who remember the evil done may be a little less liable to see it done again. More tea?

SIX HANDS

I watch for it every Easter vigil, and every Easter vigil it happens —
this Easter vigil right in front of me where I sat in the second row
of the chapel expressly to see it; and once again I nearly burst into
tears, because it's so beautiful and subtle and gentle and heartrend-
ing and amazing, and you would totally miss it if you were not watching closely for it.

So here, sit with me and watch as the candidates for Confirmation come up the aisle shyly, smiling and nervous and beaming,
and their sponsors come up behind them, and the twelve men and
women arrange themselves on the steps of the altar, the sponsors one
step higher than the candidates, and Father John says something joyous which I don't quite catch, because *there it is!* — the sponsors ever
so gently, so affectionately, so proudly, putting their right hands on
the right shoulders of the candidates! and four of the six candidates
reaching their left hands up and put their hands on their sponsors'
hands! and the fifth candidate from the right laughing and weeping
at once, a lovely sight. You can see the sheen of tears sliding down her
face and you never saw tears that were so absolutely not sad as those
tears.

Father John then talks passionately from his huge honest genuine heart about how this is not only an extraordinary moment for the
candidates and their families and their sponsors but also for us as a
community, because we have six new members and they have worked
hard and long to be here in this thrilling holy moment and when he
has finished anointing them with oil, and praying for them, and confirming them as members of the Church, with all the rights and privileges and responsibilities thereunto, he hopes that we will stand and
extend an uproarious welcome and applaud these brave souls who
have chosen to step into the grace which resides in the Church, the
Church being no mere structure or corporate entity but all of us gath-

ered around the world at sweet holy shivering moments like this one.

Father John then booms out prayers and makes his way down the line of the candidates, anointing them and confirming them and blessing them and hugging them and their sponsors, and we all sit in our pews smiling and laughing at the relaxed burble of it all, and then when Father John is done he turns and presents the six new members of our community with a wave of his hand just like a stage manager presents the terrific cast of the wonderful play, and we all stand and applaud uproariously, with the sort of whistles and cheering you would hear after a delicious victory, which this is, when you think about it.

But all through Father John's passionate speech and prayers and anointing, I watched the sponsors and their right hands. All six of the sponsors kept their right hands on the right shoulders of their candidates for the longest time, as long as they possibly could, I think, lifting them off only to hug Father John and applaud their candidates at the end, and there's something about the way those hands rested so proudly, so gently, so lovingly on the shoulders of the candidates that gives me the shivering happy willies when I think about it. Such tiny things mean so very much, don't they? The little things that are not little at all. All that love and pride and trust and delight and hope, all caught by a hand shyly reaching out and coming to rest on the shoulder of another person at an extraordinary moment for both people, for all twelve of those people, for everyone in the chapel that evening, for everyone in the world who believes that there is such a thing as grace overwhelming you when you need it most, as hope defiant against the fleeing darkness, as love rising ever higher like an irresistible tide, as hands reaching tenderly for you when you thought all was dark and dim and always would be, but that is not so. That is not at all so.

MEIRICEÁNACH GHAELACH

The wedding was on Saturday afternoon, between an American Irish woman and an American Irish man. Both vast clans were in nearly full attendance and there was a great deal of dancing and laughing and dandling of babies. I counted four young women who were enormously pregnant and, as a priest said to me, if God is in high humor today one or more of those women will deliver during the wedding reception and we will welcome new guests to the feast.

Sunday everyone slept in and then went to late Mass.

Monday morning was the funeral of the bride's beloved bachelor uncle. More than fifty of the people who had been at the wedding were at the funeral. Three of the four pregnant women were there also and the priest said it would be good for one to deliver here because we have a lovely baptismal font in this church.

None of the pregnant women delivered during the funeral, although one of them said to me later she thought she was going to deliver right there in her pew because she was laughing so hard when the deceased uncle's nephew did a spot-on hilarious imitation of the uncle's famous soft-shoe dance while singing in pubs, which he loved to do and did very well and fairly often.

At the funeral a number of people laughed so hard they wept.

Because so many of us at the wedding and the funeral were American Irish there was Gaelic in the air and most of the older men wore the black suits that every American Irish male of a certain age has in his closet for wakes and funerals. Most of the younger men wore suits of many different colors and sheens. The priest and I noticed this and he said with a smile that it is the nature of traditions to change, this is normal and natural, and we would be foolish to gnash our teeth about the loss of the old ways, but I do like the way so many of us of a certain age are in our blacks, for I am reminded of my forebears, and that is a warm and welcome memory. We waked the dead in the old way in our family, the wake going all night long over the casket and then everyone off to Mass in the morning, several men trundling the casket down the steps of the house to the church.

There was a moment at the funeral, just after one of the pregnant women read aloud from the New Testament and before the older brother of the deceased spoke a wry and heartfelt eulogy, when a small great-niece needed to go to the crying room and her lanky father carried her down the aisle, through the massed rank of the clan of both the bride and the deceased, and as the father and the child walked down the aisle several hands, male and female, rose up to touch the man and the child, just for an instant, without any drama or even conscious intent, I think, and I stood there, in the back of the church, near the baptismal font and wept, for reasons that are not wholly clear to me even now as I try to speak them with my fingers. Life and love and death and laughter and black suits and babies on shoulders and Gaelic in the air and your beloved bachelor uncle opening his mouth to sing in the pub of a Friday evening.

It was long ago our people left Ireland, and well they should, fleeing famine and savagery at the hands of the imperialist slavemaster and finding peace and joy in America, where they were free to speak their minds and worship as they please; and not one of us at the wedding and the funeral would choose to return to the wet green rocky island from which so many of our forebears came, for our America, despite its greed and violence, is a nation unlike any other in its verve and roar, its creativity and courage, its sweep and scope, the nation where our people came to harbor after many a storm at sea; but very many of us at the wedding and the funeral these last few days were proud that we were Meiriceánach Ghaelach, American Irish, and the only thing that would have made it an even more deliciously American Irish triad of days is if two of the pregnant women had delivered their babies, one as a sudden gift to the newly married couple and one as a vigorous squalling prayer in memory of the deceased, may he rest in peace.

HOLES

Every family has a secret hole. Every family has more people at the table than you can see. If we set the right number of plates for all the people at the table we would have to build way bigger tables. No one talks about these holes, and you can understand why, because the holes never actually heal, and they are awash with tidal pain, and when you stumble into a hole again for some reason, such as a sudden photograph or an artless question, there's the pain again, patient and terrible, as ready with the scalpel as ever, and you stand there in the kitchen, holding onto the counter with both hands, trying to get your breathing back in order, wondering for the hundredth time how it is that pain like this causes you to feel as if you are suddenly hollow, with nothing at all remaining of the crucial organs that used to be behind the flimsy armor of your chest.

I have seen people stumble into their holes. I have watched it happen. You can see it happen in the countries of their faces. I saw a man look at a photograph and see the brother who wasn't in it. I saw that happen on his face. I saw a woman say *two* when someone asked her how many children she had and I realized the answer was three. I have seen a woman fall again and again into the hole where her father used to be. I saw a woman just the other day grab hold of the kitchen counter with both hands because she was walking through the kitchen with a platter of food and she slid into the hole left by her baby brother who was always her baby brother even when he died at fifty.

We try all sorts of things to hide the holes. Some people run as fast as they can for as long as they can to stay ahead of their holes. Some people build stories and live inside them. Some people construct lockboxes or complicated labyrinthine jails for their holes. Some people pour whiskey or worse in their holes. Some people get trapped in their holes and become their holes and lose themselves forever. Some people acknowledge their holes and treat them as family members you cannot evade. Some people try to bend their holes into music or paintings or essays or books. Some people pour prayers into their holes. Some people try to become other people altogether so that their holes lose track of them and wander around aimlessly without anyone to haunt.

Everyone is in a family somehow. There are all sorts of families, and all families are odd and awkward and shapeshifting, and they all have holes and people herding and huddling and hiding from those holes. But it turns out you cannot hide from your holes and they are always there somewhere inside or around you and there is nothing you can do but hold on to the kitchen counter, or reach for someone in your family, whatever kind of family that is, and wait until your crucial organs shuffle back into your hollow chest. There's nothing good about holes other than the way they make you reach for someone else, maybe at the same time that person is reaching for you; which is another one of the things we mean when we try to say what we mean by love, and God, and praying.

VIII.

BEAR MOUNTAIN

Father Paul drove us in one of the two parish cars. There were five of us boys. The parish cars were Buicks and they were huge and black. It was late September. All five of us were thirteen years old. Now that we had achieved the age of reason we were allowed to visit the seminary to begin the process of discernment. Father Paul had high hopes but low expectations. If even one of us expressed serious interest in a second visit to the seminary he would count the weekend a roaring success and no mistake, as he told the pastor. They were leaning against the car as we climbed in. The pastor was a monsignor. A monsignor was halfway between priest and bishop. We had a choice of seminaries, said Father Paul to us as we drove off. We could visit the Capuchin seminary or the Franciscan seminary. They were in the same town up on the river and both in his experience were excellent in shaping good priests.

One of us voted for the Franciscans because he had a dog and Francis loved animals and three of us voted for the Capuchins because the word Capuchin was cool. I voted for the Capuchins because my dad's best friend was a small hilarious Capuchin, so as far as I knew the Capuchins were small and hilarious and cool.

We drove through the Borough of Queens, through the Borough of the Bronx, and then north along the mighty Hudson River, which is not its original name, of course, said Father Paul. The first people here had many names for it, among them the Shatemuc, the River of the Pelicans, and Mohicanhitheck, the River of the Wolves. I have seen pelicans here, but I have not seen wolves as yet.

We stared out the window at the river and saw gulls and crows and herons and ducks and maybe a hawk but no pelicans or wolves.

Father Paul had started to talk about vocations while we were still in the Bronx but then he had wisely turned the conversation to the Mets, who had great pitching this year, for once. At Dobbs Ferry the river grew wider and you could hardly see across it to the steep wooded cliffs of the Palisades. Tarrytown, Sleepy Hollow, where the headless horseman roamed of old, Ossining, Croton Bay, Bear Mountain. The first European explorers, said Father Paul, all remarked the particular sheen of the black bears in this area; my theory is that it had to do with their diet, perhaps a rich crop of beech nuts. The staff at the seminary tells me they see a great number of bears when their apple trees are ripe, and that they do not rake up fallen apples but leave them for the bears. Perhaps you young men will see bears this weekend.

We saw a great many things that weekend, and the staff at the seminary was kindly and courteous, although much taller than the Capuchin I knew, and while one of the Capuchins in particular was refreshingly honest about the priesthood, which he said was unrewarding financially but rich in meditative opportunities and unexpected friends, none of the five of us were able to discern any inclination to explore our potential vocations and Father Paul drove us back home on Sunday afternoon. We listened to the Mets on the radio. The Mets beat the Phillies to go up eight games with two to play, and not even the Mets can lose the pennant up eight games with two to play, as Father Paul said. When the Mets got the last out we were in Yonkers and Father Paul was so pleased at the victory he stopped and bought us ice cream.

I never did discern the possibility of a vocation to the priesthood that weekend, or any other time in my long life, but there were two moments that stay with me even now about that trip — I think because they were my initial glimpses of the deeper lives of priests.

The first was when one of us shyly asked the honest Capuchin about celibacy. We were sitting at a picnic table near the apple orchard, the five of us boys and the honest Capuchin, and he was silent for a moment and then he said, In my experience celibacy is not the terrible cross to bear that everyone thinks it is; loneliness is the much heavier burden. Sometimes you do feel awfully alone. We talk about being close to God, as priests, and devoting ourselves to God's work, and consciously giving up one sort of life so as to be able to devote ourselves to another with our whole heart and mind, but to be honest there are a lot of times when you are just really lonely. I don't want to mislead you about that. You try to face it straight, is all I can say. I try to stay active. I walk in the woods a great deal when it comes. Sometimes I drive down to Bear Mountain and walk there for a while. Indeed there are bears on Bear Mountain, and a remarkable number of owls. An enterprising naturalist would study the owls on Bear Mountain to see how the mountain can support such a population. But every priest has to develop his own way to grapple with the loneliness. I think sometimes that's what the story of Jacob and the angel is about. I don't want to scare you off about this, but I do want to be honest. For every additional grace a priest is granted by virtue of his vocation there is a price to pay, is what I am trying to say. But then I have only been a priest for ten years. I often think only a priest with fifty years of experience can say anything true about being a priest. Although interestingly it's the oldest priests who are usually the ones who smile and say they don't have anything wise to say about being a priest. Humility is the final frontier for us all, as a friend of mine says. Not even Jesus thought He was cool, as my friend says. Something to remember. You guys hungry?

The other moment was in Yonkers, at the ice-cream shop, when we got back in Father Paul's car and we all sat for a moment working on our cones and making sure they didn't drip on the pristine interior of the parish Buick. It was late afternoon and it had been a hot day and we had rolled down all the windows. Father Paul had taken off his jacket and rolled up his sleeves and he was happily working on a strawberry cone. You could tell he was genuinely pleased about the Mets and his ice cream cone and the way the river was glinting with sailboats. Just for a second you could see that he was a regular guy who couldn't *believe* that the Mets who had been so comically awful for seven years since they were born as essentially a joke were about to win the National League pennant by eight games, beating all those old famous teams, and that he absolutely loved strawberry ice cream from a place that made it fresh themselves, and that he loved driving along the river and talking about bears. You could tell that he actually liked driving guys up to the seminary and back and that while he vaguely hoped one of us might have the itch he knew it was unlikely and he wasn't overly disappointed that he was zero for five with this group. You could see that he actually liked being a priest, and that to him it was a cool thing to be, but he didn't think it didn't make him holier or more important than anyone else. You got a sense that he was priest because he wanted to try to reach some deep thing that he couldn't explain, a thing that he could only get at by saying yes to a job that was rewarding in some ways and really hard in some other ways.

On our way through the Bronx one of us said something about the Yankees, who played in the Bronx, and Father Paul laughed and said, The poor Yankees are going to finish about thirty games behind the Orioles this year, boys. In fact even the Senators are going to finish ahead of the Yankees. There are *college* teams that are better than the Yankees this year. This is a great year. I cast no aspersions on Yankee fans, because it would be wrong to revel in the bitter disappointment of your fellow beings, but we *can* certainly enjoy the rare treat of a great year for the Mets, and this beautiful afternoon in New York, and the fact that there is strawberry ice cream in this world. I'd stop for more ice cream, because there's a miraculous gelato shop in Queens, but I promised your parents we would be home by dark and so we will, boys, so we will.

THE SPECIAL COLLECTION

Watching the collection baskets circulate this morning at Mass, I am suddenly and powerfully reminded of an extraordinary moment from my childhood.

Sit with me then, at the noon Mass on Sunday, the last Mass, the one that collects all the sleepy teenagers grimly attending the Mass they do *not* want to attend and have bickered *continually* about attending and are grimly attending only because of some faint shard of remnant respect for their parents, like a last good seed in a pile of husks.

I am one of those teenagers, slumped in the back, yawning, annoyed, bored, resentful, absorbed only by the occasional thumping of headlong bees against the stained-glass windows; do they think the brightly colored saints are mountainous flowers?

The collection begins; the two ushers start their mathematical progression from the front pews to the back; surely I am not the only cynical teenager silently excoriating the commercial pause, the rustle of lucre, the ostentatious deposits of big bills and fat envelopes, the scrabble of money in the temple, all in the name of the One who lost His temper for this very reason in a temple long ago and started a memorable ruckus about it; and I sneer at the naked greed of it all.

And then there is a moment.

One of the two ushers distributing the collection baskets is named John. He is the janitor at the school attached to the church. He has been the janitor for as long as anyone can remember. He is about five feet tall. He is famously gruff and grumpy. He was born in Italy. His hands and forearms look like steel cables. He has cleaned up everything you can possibly imagine spilled in the school. Go ahead and imagine what he spent years cleaning up. During the week he wears blue jeans and a blue denim shirt and work boots and he is never still. He also is the gardener and the mechanic and the electrician and the plumber for the school and the church and the rectory and the convent. I never saw him smile in the years I was a boy in school and church there. I do not know if he was married or a dad or a grandfather or solitary or bruised or a mystic. We children took him for granted. He was just there. When something went wrong he fixed it without comment. He wasn't friendly or unfriendly, just terse. Maybe he didn't speak our language very well and didn't want to make mistakes in it. Maybe he didn't like his work even though he had done it forever. We didn't know. We didn't know anything about him. He was just there. When something went wrong he fixed it and then rattled away with his bucket and mops and his face of glower and granite.

But this morning, when the ushers finish the collection and leave their baskets at the foot of the altar and bow and turn to slip back into the alcove, the celebrant stops John, with a hand on his shoulder, and he and John stand there, as the other usher retrieves two new baskets, and the priest says, in his booming voice, that this is John's final Mass as usher, that he is retiring after an astounding *fifty* years of service to the parish, and that he is returning to his ancestral home to be with his extended family.

As many of you know, booms the celebrant, John has served our church, and our school, and the priests and nuns of this parish, with admirable patience and diligence in every conceivable capacity, and the fact is that our entire parish, for many long years, has rested on the broad shoulders of this gracious man, to whom we are most grateful, and to whom we owe our heartfelt thanks. So this morning I will ask two favors of you all. We will take up a special collection for John, as a parting gift and thanks for his extraordinary generosity, and we will applaud this good man, who gave of himself to others without complaint, in the exact spirit of Our Lord Jesus Christ.

I suppose now that the collection baskets for John filled to overflowing. I suppose now, if I were to calculate how many people were there and how moved most of us were, that finally there were thousands of dollars in the baskets. I saw several men hurriedly writing checks, and when the basket came to me I saw lots of twenty-dollar bills, more than I had ever seen before; and I felt awful that I had nothing to add.

But it's not the overflowing baskets I remember clearest from that moment. It's the two men standing at the front of the church. The pastor never took his hand off John's shoulder and both men stood there with a sheen of tears on their faces and neither man moved under the storm of applause from the congregation, and only when the two new baskets were carried up to the altar, by two men of the Nocturnal Adoration Society, did the priest hug John and John turn and hurriedly walk back into the shadows of the alcove, almost ducking from the applause. I remember that he looked at the floor as he walked and didn't wave or smile or anything like that. Still, it seems to me, that was one of the most joyous moments I ever saw in our Church, and I will never forget it, and perhaps now you will not forget it either.

SHOULDERING

One of the best things about having a lot of brothers is not something that people with lots of brothers talk about much, but I think we should speak of it this morning, for I miss it, and I doubt I will ever feel it again in quite the same way, and it mattered enormously to me and somehow contributed to making me who I am in all sorts of ways, so let us think for a moment about brushing up against the bulk of brothers in the kitchen, and bumping gently into brothers in the hallway, and being crammed against brothers in the back seats of cars, and standing shoulder-to-shoulder with brothers in basketball games and tense moments, and having the arms and legs of brothers draped over you like thick vines and cables as you sprawl on floors and couches and beaches, and having a brother's chin suddenly plopped on your left shoulder from behind as you sleepily make coffee.

Things like that.

We talk about collisions and battles and fisticuffs and hugs and handshakes and sharp elbows when we talk about lots of brothers, and well we should, because you cannot have a lot of brothers and not crash into them in every imaginable way including sometimes headfirst, both with and without helmets, and sometimes we talk about the gentler brotherly touches, like a big eloquent hand on your shoulder when you desperately need a large tender hand on your shoulder, or a huge hand extended to help you up when you are down and dazed, or the way that bigger brothers hold the hands of littler brothers sometimes, which every time I see that I cry at such a shimmer of love right there in front of me at the bus stop or the train station or the schoolyard or the chapel, but we hardly talk about the slight brotherly brushes, the wordless hey of a brother deliberately leaning into you for no reason whatsoever as he shuffles past with his sandwich and tea. That's a way to say I love you. Yes it is. There are a lot of ways to say I love you, it turns out, and two brothers cheerfully shouldering a third brother away from the plate of cookies and deftly boxing him out without undue effort even as he sets his feet and tries to leverage his way through and they are all grinning is an excellent way to say I love you, and I miss that, I miss that fiercely this morning.

Just for a moment to shuffle back into the kitchen sleepy and discombobulated and instantly be confronted with a gentle elbow to the throat would be immeasurably sweet; and then an ever-so-infinitesimal hip check; and then when I reach for the bacon a massive form interrupts and I find myself reaching for air, and I hear several large men chortling, one of whom is our dad, who is the captain of the bacon, and if you think you are going to move him out of his front-row seat by the stove, not to mention he has the epic old spatula and he knows how to use it, you have another think coming, young man, although every one of his sons this morning will shoulder up against the chieftain, and lean strenuously against his brothers, and in a moment our mom will come in and glare wordlessly and we will get the message and retreat to the table like civilized beings, but just for one last delicious instant I lean against one large brother, and a taller thinner brother is leaning on us two, and the biggest of us all is leaning on the three younger brothers, and we are all leaning on the chieftain, who is laughing but immovable, and the bacon is almost done, and if you listen carefully you can hear all five men in the kitchen chortling gently.

URGES

I am nine years old and in fourth grade. I am the youngest kid in the class, as usual. This is my parents' fault, as an older boy explains gently. If your parents had timed their urges properly you would be ten years old.

I think about my parents' urges for a while. Their foremost urges are to read so many magazines and newspapers that we younger kids have to shovel paths through them on Saturdays, occasionally forgetting to clear a path for our youngest brother Tommy so that he has sometimes been trapped for days at a time, eating grubs and drinking rainwater he collects in bottle-caps; for we are not allowed to shovel paths on Sunday, and from Monday through Friday we are busy with school, unless you hear a plaintive cry that for a while you think is a squirrel with rickets but then realize is Tommy and we shovel him out, checking his pockets for grubs.

Our oldest brother has the urge for higher mathematics, which is why he is so thin, says our dad: Mathematics is an attenuating pursuit, unlike theology, which is voluminous — ever see a painting of Thomas Aquinas? Trust me, there are no small paintings of Thomas Aquinas.

This is how our dad talks, with a new and riveting idea in every sentence.

Our sister has the urge to listen to folk music, which our dad says has to do with roundelay singing, which is disturbing, like Calvinism. She also has the urge to be a professional clown, but the main political parties are not hiring this year, says our dad, so she will have to wait on that one or go to San Francisco and work on her game in the minor leagues there.

I say to the older boy who explained about urges, how did *your* parents time their urges?, and he says do you want a punch in the nose?, and I say no, thank you, as I was brought up to say by my parents, and he then goes on at great length about punching people and I realize that he has a powerful urge to punch someone and it probably will not matter much to him who it is, so I wait for a lull in the flow of his talk, and disengage politely, as I was taught to do in moments of public idiocy, and I make my way home, and start in on my theology homework, for I wish to gain a few pounds and no longer look like an exclamation point with spectacles, as our dad says, but then I hear a faint plaintive warble, as if a cricket was singing Hank Williams, and I recruit a brother to join me in digging a path for Tommy, who says he has been up there since Easter but that he is okay, because he ate a praying mantis, which is a species of animal in which the female eats the head of the male after their urges are satisfied, which is a powerful metaphor for something we do not understand, says our dad, which is an excellent definition of the word theology.

USHERING

In my parish, as perhaps in yours, there are two cool calm efficient souls who lurk around the last pews on either side of the church at the last crowded morning Mass. Their task, these two brisk and gently commanding souls, is to direct stragglers to unoccupied seats so that the stragglers do not just slouch around in the rear of the church, obstructing the doors and crowding the corners and clogging the sight lines of the weary young parents in the crying room; instead they are seated as full members of the congregation, participating in the ancient beloved ritual of the Mass, and not *slogging around hugging the walls like teenagers at a dance,* as one of the two calm efficient souls said to me after Mass yesterday.

I asked her what she thinks about as she does her work at Mass and she said, First and foremost, silence. I never say a word. I try to use gentle gestures. I try to remember that I am a servant of the faithful here and you cannot bark or snap at someone even though you very much want to do just that sometimes. Second, I am very sensitive to not being in the way. The Mass is sacred and I don't want to distract anyone. I would feel awful if that happened.

The job is to slip people into open spaces as quickly and quietly and courteously as possible. People tend to sit at the ends of the pews and leave big empty spaces in the middle, and people also have personal space bubbles, you know, so that a group will leave at least two spaces between them and the next group if they can. I suppose it's some ancient mammalian thing, to leave defensive space or something. And then families *sprawl.* Young families sprawl the most. Young families start out with the parents at either end of the group and the children in the middle, until the wrestling or complaining starts, and then the dad will insert himself between kids. It's always the dad on defense. You notice a lot, watching people.

The busiest time is the first ten minutes of Mass, as you would expect, but people do drift in for the first twenty minutes. Yes, there are a few people who come in just before the consecration and leave just after, but I don't try to seat them. They don't want to sit. With them and with people who are really late, I try to remember that hey, they made it to Mass, and who knows why they are late? Maybe they had a very good reason indeed to be late and they are at Mass because they need Mass desperately and who am I to get sniffy about their punctuality?

It's interesting to me that an awful lot of people still prefer to sit in the back of church rather than even in the middle, let alone up front. I think it's left over from when they were kids in school and the back of the room was furthest from the teacher. Some people want to sit right up front, either for hearing purposes or sometimes, to be honest, maybe to show off a little, but people who want to sit up close will do so on their own and they don't need my help. I focus on helping people find seats quickly and calmly so they can focus on Mass. Mostly I am just looking to get people seated quickly and smoothly but, yes, sometimes I suggest seats based on other factors. If there's someone alone in a pew I try to put other people in the pew with them. This is not a dating service, but sometimes I have put singles in with singles, yes. Do I know of any marriages resulting from my help? No.

After the first ten minutes or so most of my work is done, other than the collection. My fellow usher and I have picked out a family to bring up the gifts, and after that we are essentially finished, although both of us keep an eye out for anyone who needs help — a medical emergency, or a loose toddler, that sort of thing. You would be surprised how often there's a free-range toddler.

Being an usher doesn't get in the way of me savoring Mass, no — oddly I feel like I am more attentive and more appreciate since I started serving as an usher. I am *engaged* more. And there's something... well, poignant is a good word, about being so involved with people. I see the congregation in a different way — tall, short, old, young, having trouble walking, shy, troubled, maybe brand new to this church or this Mass. We use words like congregation and community of the faithful, but it's just all of us, you know? It's just us. So when I find room for a young couple with their two little kids in a pew between families I know have been coming for thirty years, somehow that's a good thing, that they'll all shake hands and smile at the Sign of Peace, and maybe chat a little after Mass, and be able to recognize each other next week. Isn't that what we mean by community and congregation, that we're all basically teammates?

Occasionally people say thanks after Mass, yes, but mostly not and, as my fellow usher says, that's the way it should be. We should be an invisible service, just helping people savor Mass. The Mass is a great thing. We take it a little for granted, I think. We take for granted that it's available all day, every day, somewhere. I try to remember that there are still places where Mass is a crime and you can be imprisoned and executed for it. And even in those places people will do incredibly brave things to be able to witness Mass. It's a shocking miracle, the Mass. We forget that. *I* forget it sometimes and find myself going through the motions, and then I'll snap awake and remember that this is a mysterious and amazing thing that can heal and save people, really and truly. I know people who have been starving for something and they came to Mass and found what they were starving for. Fact. That's what I try to remember, when I am ushering — that my job is not really to find seats; it's to silently and gently help bring people closer to the miracle of the Mass. Pretty cool job.

THE LANGUAGE OF HIS BODY

It was my older brother Kevin who taught me to play chess. We sprawled on the nap of the old carpet, propped on our elbows, his legs behind him as long as a week. He didn't explain theory or strategy or history or anything like that. We just played and he beat me again and again and again and again. I suppose you could say he beat me mercilessly, for never once did he let me replay a move, never once did he wink and allow something to happen, never once did he miss a move he knew I saw. When I made an egregious mistake he would silently take advantage of it and then continue to stare at the board, utterly absorbed in the geometry and narrative and currents and possibilities of the game. When I slowly began to make good moves and then, even more slowly, inventive and creative and devious ones, he would occasionally go so far as to cock an eyebrow at what I had startlingly accomplished; but that infinitesimal gesture, the subtle flicker of a tiny muscle over his left eye, was as far as he would go toward issuing praise.

Kevin was a quiet man even when young, and you never met a man who was less fulsome or garrulous or logorrheic or profligate with the words that came out of his mouth. Yet he could and did express himself with wonderful clarity if you were so lucky as to be trained in reading the language of his body. I think he wanted me to learn the game by being *in* the game, by watching what he did and ascertaining why, by testing my own growing confidence and creativity against his, even though he was eight years older and the nature of my education was to be beaten again and again and again and again for weeks before I began to challenge him, here and there, and then to actually contest games, and then to press him hard, and then force him to the peak of his powers simply to fend me off, and finally to beat him.

I wish now I could remember the day and the hour and the

angle of light and who else was in the room and if he finally looked up from the board and smiled his slight wry smile which to me and our sister and brothers was a huge vast smile if you were so lucky as to understand the language of his body. It wasn't that he was actually stern or somber or baleful as some people thought when confronted with the unyielding flint of his face; it was that he was a quiet man even when young, and a slight gesture in him was a broad gesture in another.

I would guess that what happened that day was that it was late in the afternoon in that last languorous hour before dinner and we were sprawled on the nubby russet carpet and probably it was summer and soon he would be off to college and the Navy; and we had played a terrific swirling game in which my bishops had slashed here and there with grim abandon; and while he grew absorbed in murderous plots against my reckless churchmen, my horsemen had quietly built a jail from which he could not escape, using his own pawns as tiny walls; and when one of my own pawns shyly shuffled forward a single space and thus shivered the geometry of the board in such a way that my brother had no recourse but to surrender.

There were a few long silent moments for which I cannot, even all these years later, find good words. We lay there staring at the board, and his legs went on forever, and both of us knew the weight and freight of the moment, and then maybe he looked up at me and smiled that slight wry smile, which to me was like a trumpet or a burst of song; and then we went to dinner.

THE IMPOSSIBLE POSSIBLE

We had not one but two baptisms at Mass the other day, and while there were many moving and entertaining moments therein — for example one moppet squalling steadily in the key of C throughout the entire ceremony, a remarkable operatic performance, and the other child, as round of visage as the later Orson Welles, sleeping through the entire ceremony, not even flickering awake when the tall priest marked her with oil and then poured water into her tiny black Mohawk haircut — what absorbed me after a while was the way little kids edged toward the event like avid eager wasps to a summer picnic.

Yes, the tall priest had welcomed the children up to the altar, booming out his baritone invitation and waving his arms like railroad crossing gates, and a few kids had shot up the aisle instantly like falcons with ponytails, and then a few more edged out from the wings of the church and sat down crosslegged and fascinated too; but it was the next few minutes that riveted me, for even as the priest went to work at the baptistery, and the parents and godparents stood there blinking and beaming, and several people in the congregation hummed along with the kid wailing steadily in the key of C, and I realized that the other baby looked *exactly* like Joe Strummer when he had a Mohawk in the last year the Clash were great, little kids kept edging out of the pews, and sliding surreptitiously toward the altar, and crouching behind the pillars at either side of the nave, and peering out amazed and delighted as the two babies were oiled and washed in the waters of the Lord.

I watched one boy, maybe age four, slip out of his pew and plaster himself against the wall, looking uncannily like a tiny cat burglar, and slowly melt along the wall toward the altar, grinning at those of us who grinned at him. I bet it took him five minutes to go twenty pews along that wall, but the priest was being expansive and garrulous and relaxed about pacing, so by the time the priest got to the actual baptizing of the squaller and the sleeper, the cat burglar had achieved the end of the wall, near the pillar where I counted four other kids crouched and wary and absorbed.

Most essays about baptisms would pause here to say something piercing about baptism, and how clans and tribes have been christening their startled children in fresh clean water for a million years, and how gathering in community to bless a new being with prayer and laughter is a thing far bigger than the word *holy* can carry, and how what we mean by sacrament is so often exactly this sort of gathering to pray at a project launch, but I want to stay with the little kids running and tiptoeing and sneaking up on the sacred and watching with awe, crouched behind the pillars and sitting crosslegged on the steps of the altar, and plastered to the wall where it ends near the chancel.

We all sprint or tiptoe toward the sacred, thrilled and hesitant and awed and skeptical but unable to sustain cynicism or denial, for we know somehow somewhere deep inside that yes, there *is* sacred, and yes, there *are* miracles extant and possible far beyond our ken, and yes, we *are* shards and aspects of the divine in ways we will never understand, and yes, when we gather together some reminder, some gently opening window, some wriggle of stunning *is* possible; and that is why we go to church, isn't it? That is why we belong to religions, and attend services, and savor sacramental moments, because there might be a rush of sudden water that washes away despair and refills our hope capacitors when we thought they were forever dust and echo. We are all small shy cat burglars edging toward the sacred, thrilled and scared; we are all that boy, unable to resist the impossible possible.

THE RUDE BURL OF OUR MASKS

One day when I was twelve years old and setting off on my newspaper route after school my mom said *will you stop at the doctor's and pick up something for me* and I grimaced and said something almost rude but not all the way rude and off I went on my bicycle.

In autumn where we lived, the afternoon didn't slide gently or melt easily into dusk but just snarled and surrendered and suddenly everything went brown.

My mom had lost interior parts one after another over the years, but I knew nothing and cared nothing of which parts and why and how they had been lost.

I had sixty papers to deliver and I could deliver them in exactly seventy minutes if all went well, but now I would have to go easily five whole minutes out of my way all the way over by the woods by the highway and I would not get home until long after five o'clock which meant I would miss most of the one television show we were allowed to watch per day. How my mom could be so thoughtless about this matter was a mystery to me.

I delivered my papers as fast as I could, sometimes riding my bicycle over lawns and once right up porch steps.

My mom never explained what interior parts she was missing or where they went or how painful and complicated it was to live without certain of your crucial interior parts, for example not being able to eat certain foods.

By the time I got to the doctor's office the world was browning so fast it was like someone huge was exhaling brown at a herculean rate.

My mom never complained about anything, even when she had to lie down for a whole day or even two sometimes and we had to be as quiet as we could possibly be, which meant take your fistfight outside or else.

I knocked on the door of the doctor's office and no one answered and I knocked again and no one answered and I said something unforgivably rude for which I still feel ashamed of myself even today although no one heard me in the deep brown dusk near the woods by the highway.

Sometimes my mom would vanish for a few days and the stern glare of our grandmother was in charge until our dad came home from the city and we would be so happy to see him that we leapt off the porch and sprinted to the corner and burbled home with him pretending that we too wore fedora hats and cool brown overcoats.

Finally an older woman in some sort of medical tunic opened the door and I explained that I was picking up something for my mom and here is her name and here is the envelope with the money and thank you and off I went on my bicycle. The quickest way home at that point was to cut through the woods by the highway.

My mom could be tart and terse and curt and sharp and sometimes she bit and snapped words so that your ear stung, but when she put her long calm brown fingers on your neck or shoulder all was well and all manner of things was well.

The woods were so black and brawly with branch and scatter that I got off my bicycle and walked through the sifting darkness.

When I got home I handed her the package and she said thanks and I said something not rude for once and even now all these years later I wish I would have said a thousand thousand more gentle reverent things to my mother than I ever did in the years we lived together in that house by the woods by the highway.

But we hardly ever say the things we ought to say, and desperately wish to say, from under the rude burl of our masks, even now.

IX.

THEY

They arise from their beds at about nine in the morning. Their beds are close enough that they can each lie abed and hold hands across the narrow abyss if necessary. They breakfast together and they share the marmalade and the tea and the newspapers, as they have done since they were married more than seventy years ago. They parse and divvy the newspapers according to a system they invented in the brief months they lived together as a young married couple in a rooming house while he prepared to enter the war against those who would enslave the world.

They attend to correspondence and social matters and household matters and sundry other matters, some of which entail them driving hither and yon to pray or play or be prodded by learned doctors, and then they share a light repast, and then they nap, for one of the best things about being in your tenth decade of life, they say, is that you are allowed to close up shop for two hours in the hot afternoon and peel down to your skivvies and take a nap, which is a delicious thing, all things considered, and almost always serves to recharge the system for their evening ramble, during which they dine with their son and his family and tell tall tales and remember past adventures and escapades and relate the stories of the day, which may include correspondence of various sorts with their other sons and daughter and grandsons and granddaughters but not as yet their great-grandson, who cannot yet deftly handle a pencil but soon will be of an age to burble into the telephone about the excellent huge slobbery dog he licked today or the remarkable number of olives he crammed up his nose as a botanical experiment or the sparrow who invited him to lunch in the most courteous manner.

Then they make their way to their couch, around which are stacks and piles and gaggles of books and magazines and newspapers, in which they swim with sharp interest and long erudition, for they both are literate and literary people, himself the author of two books and long a newspaperman, and herself the author of a meticulous and astonishing family chronicle, into which a reader can dip anywhere and find the angle of winter sunlight, for example, in the Bronx in 1930 or the cadence of a nun's voice in 1937 in Brooklyn or the first cry of a baby in 1946, the year the sergeant came home gaunt from the war, amazed to be alive.

Then they may watch some television, although often they flip it on but do not notice it at all, nor hear it, as they mute it instantly to obviate the natter and yawp, and only glance at the screen here and there to see who is winning the tennis tournament and note if this new golden youth is anywhere near as graceful as the golden youths of the past.

Then they yawn, one after another, and remove their spectacles and make their way slowly to their beds; but before they sleep there is a slight gentle ordinary extraordinary moment that mostly no one sees but I have seen, several times, and often remember with emotions so swirling and deep that I cannot find words for them. They pause, just inside the doorway of their bedroom, and they kiss, as they have done since they were married more than seventy years ago; and then my mother folds her walker and slips into bed and my father slips into his bed; and every once in a while, for no reason either of them could explain, they reach across the narrow space between their beds and hold hands, just for a moment, before they sleep.

COULD I HAVE A WORD WITH YOU?

This was what our dad would say when he was annoyed or seeth-ing, and his children all learned early to interpret those seven words, always spoken quietly and calmly, as incipient doom and looming penalty, which generally meant being sent to your room; funny how being in your room was refuge and relaxation except when you were *confined* to it, at which point suddenly it was a beautifully painted prison cell from which you stared longingly into the back yard, where your brothers would be capering and making vulgar gestures and mooning you and savoring every moment of your period of incar-ceration, in much the same fashion as sparrows taunt a housebound cat; though the cat takes careful notes as to faces and stores up his resentment on small interior shelves designed just for this purpose.

You would be walking briskly through the house, having just committed brotherly battery, and sensibly wishing to get as far from the scene of the incident as possible, and there would be our tall silent dad, sitting in his brown chair by the brown radio, and just as you thought you were clear, and loosed into the hallway to choose among several excellent escape options, you would hear him say *could I have a word with you?,* and even though he said it so quietly that you would think no one more than a few inches away from him would catch it, you would be thoroughly wrong about that, for his words rang in the air with a clarion shout and you instantly froze in place and all brothers within hundreds of yards also froze, thinking for a second that those words had come for them and they were totally and completely screwed; but no, those seven words were for you and you alone, my lad, and you turned slowly and sat down on the brown couch and your dad leaned in gently and said something quietly; and then you went to your room for a thousand years.

He hit me once, our dad, and I deserved it, having driven drunk in the only car we had, but even then it was a short sharp sudden slap to wake me up to the depth of his anger and fear and to the danger in which I had put myself and our family and dozens of innocents on the road; and he hit our oldest brother once, and by all accounts our oldest brother eminently deserved it; but I do not think he ever, before or after those incidents, struck another of his several children, or roared at us, or even spoke sharply.

Somehow, even with all those children, and with the usual brawl and bawl among his sons, and what surely must have been many a snide remark from his daughter, our dad never lost his temper, or even, that we remember, his equanimity; and just as amazing, he never seemed to miss a crime or misdemeanor but somehow knew of it instantly and was there in his brown chair waiting to quietly say *could I have a word with you?* as soon as your guilty face hove into view.

I have roared at my children; I have shouted at them with such vehemence that the veins bulged in my neck and the dog cowered in the corner; I have had the urge to strike a son, but by merciful miracle did not; I have barked at them, and snarled at them, and made cutting and snide remarks to them, and belittled their choices and their opinions, and for all of this I feel a constant silent private simmering shame that I have not been quite as good a father as I so desperately wanted to be, and might be even yet, given more effort and humility on my part; but I often am glad to realize that I know I have not been the best father I could be because my own father was and, to his credit and my joy, still is.

NOT TODAY

At Mass this morning there were just as many priests as there were souls in the pews, three of each, and the celebrant, to his cheerful credit, immediately herded the congregation up to the front row.

This is not fifth grade, where you sit in the back as far away from the teacher as possible, he said. This is the Mass, in which there is a *miracle,* and we should sit as close to a miracle as possible, don't you think? Would you stand as far away as possible from a baby being born, or would you get as close as you can, within reason, to witness and help celebrate the miracle? Well, then.

The three priests took turns with the readings from the Old and New Testaments — The Testimonies, as one priest friend of mine calls them — and we in the front row chanted the responses and prayers, our voices reedy in the echoing chapel and then, as the celebrant prepared for the Eucharist, he shepherded the entire congregation up to the altar and around the table.

Really and truly the Mass is a miracle, and I think we take it for granted a lot, but not today, he said. Today we six are going to slow down and watch carefully and think about what is happening and why. That man was God, yes, He was, and He gave Himself to us; He shared Himself with us, and He still does, every day, in Masses all over the world. Think about it — there must be something like a million Masses being celebrated today, in cities and forests and war zones, and on islands and boats, and in prisons and hospices, in schools and hospitals, in fields and basements and cellars and cathedrals, and every single one of those Masses has this moment, which we often maybe take for granted, but not today.

And he blessed the bread and wine, and elevated the Cup, and elevated the Host; and he knelt abashed before the glory and mystery of the miracle; and we knelt too, or most of us did, except the man who once was a Marine in the war and cannot kneel anymore; and one of the concelebrant priests deftly rang the bells, not too loud, not too soft.

Think of it, said the priest after he had distributed the bread and the wine to us. There are six of us here, half of the original twelve souls who witnessed the first Mass, upstairs in a locked room, a simple meal before the rage and tumult of the next day. Twelve then, six today. Maybe you think there really ought to be more people here at morning Mass, but *I* think it is delightful, in a way, for us to be a small and fervent community for a few moments, and that's what it's all about, isn't it? To gather in His name, and share bread and wine and story, and pause and pray for a few moments, amid the rage and tumult?

So the Mass is ended, he concluded, and we will go in peace to love and serve the Lord we will find in every heart; but we will go forth today remembering that we were *blessed* this morning to witness a *miracle*, we lucky few. The world is filled with miracles, more than we could ever count, more than we will ever know, and that is all the work of the Merciful One, the creator of all, the profligate imagination that breathed all things into being; but one of those good things is the sacrament of the Mass, which sometimes we take a little for granted — but not today, my friends. Not today.

THE SPARROW CHICK

One of the ugliest most beautiful things I ever saw in this life was a week-old sparrow chick which fell from its nest inside our ancient garage and hit the ancient concrete floor and died. I was eleven years old. My brother Tommy found it and came running for me. He was four years old. He was sobbing. We stared at the chick, or what used to be a chick, if you think that the spark inside the chick makes up a lot of what the chick is, or was. It was so ugly you could not begin to explain how ugly it was, although a good start would be the scraggle of stumpy feathers and the head too big for the body and the awful stubs of wings and the gaping shattered beak and one eye missing altogether, probably eaten by another creature which probably was watching us balefully from the shadows. I said I thought it was a sparrow and Tommy said reasonably enough how do you know and I confessed I did not know, but I checked through books later and concluded that it was probably a house sparrow, though it had been born in the garage. Its naked skull was cracked just like an egg cracks when you crack it on the rim of a bowl and the shell cracks slightly jaggedly along lines of its own devising. Tommy wanted to pick it up and bury it but I said no, who knows what disease it might have had and if you get some weird disease from touching it our mom will send us to our rooms for months and we will miss summer.

A wise or deft essay would pivot gently right here and slip quietly into spiritual imagery and speculation, but Tommy and I got a piece of cardboard and slid the wreckage of the sparrow into a hole behind the garage and patted down the soil gently and scattered some grass and leaves over it so coyotes and cougars and Mrs. Erickson's evil one-eyed cat would not find and gobble it. We thought about burying it along the side of the garage where our mom had her horrifying compost pile where our oldest brother said some of the rotten vegetables did not compost but instead mutated and then waited patiently with guile to ensnare prey. This was an excellent example of evolution in action said our brother and if you don't believe me ask our dad.

I wanted to say something quiet and wise and tender to Tommy about the dead sparrow chick, but I could not find anything at all to say, not even something insipid. He had stopped sobbing but he was shuddering a little every couple of minutes as if there were sobs still inside him coming out slow and shy like they were the little brothers of the bigger sobs and were last in line and had to make sure it was okay to come out finally. I was old enough to want to say a lot of things to my brother right then, but I did not have words for what I wanted to say, so finally as we were sitting there staring at the grave I just grabbed him and hauled him in and we sat there hugging each other in the way that brothers do which is absolutely heartfelt as long as no one says anything or sees you hugging. If someone came along just then and said hey are you hugging we would both have leapt up and said what! no! of course not! do you want a punch in the eye! But we actually were hugging with all our hearts, yes we were, even though someone else would have said it's just a dead bird.

I can still feel my little brother against my chest, shuddering every couple of minutes as the last of his sobs came out slow and shy. I can feel him shuddering under my chin right now, and see the tiny muddy grave with the poor little goblin in it and feel the surly wind through the hedge behind the garage. In a minute we will get up and walk into the house hand in hand, but not quite yet. Not quite yet.

MY GRADE-SCHOOL TEACHERS

First grade: Sister Marie Aimee, with forearms like Popeye and a smile so subtle and alluring that half the boys in class thought she had been the model for the painting of the Moaning Lisa done by Leo Nardo; the other half of the boys were terrified of Sister Marie, who could and did hoist disrespectful boys into the air by gripping their shirt fronts with one hand and flicking her wrist seemingly without effort or strain; she did this once, the first week of class, with a surly boy named Michael, and then again a week later, with a heavier boy named Herman, and after that she did not need to hoist us, as a sharp glance would suffice to quell hubbub and burble instantly. The girls adored her and four of them said they were going to be nuns when they were older but I am not sure that happened.

Second grade: Mrs. Adams. The very definition of stern and foreboding and even grim on the outside, but gentle and thoughtful behind the somber mask. She made sure every one of us could read. Another teacher with a withering glare, not unlike the sudden blinding bolt of light from a lighthouse with a rotating light; I remember that she would turn slowly, like a deck gun tracking an enemy plane, and slide her glare over gaping innocents until she identified the culprit, and then she loosed the full glare. One time she left it on a boy named Timmy slightly too long and his eyeglasses heated up and singed his eyebrows, but he had thick bushy eyebrows like caterpillars and you hardly noticed the difference unless you had seen what had happened.

Third grade: Sister Rose Margaret. We thought she was a thousand years old and had personally known Pope Leo, the last pope to be elected pope without being a priest first; he was hurriedly ordained the day *after* he was elected pope, a sort of post-poping, said our dad, not to mention that he was also appointed bishop of Rome the day *after* he had been made pope of the entire church, a remarkable couple of days in the poor man's life, and this during a period when he already *had* a job, as superintendent of schools in Rome. So if any fool ever says to you that teachers do not work hard, you tell them the story of Pope Leo the Eighth.

Fourth grade: No kidding, Miss Appletree, although later she told us that she used another form of the name, Appelbaum, when she was not in school with us; that would be Miss Crannúll if she spoke the ancient language of our people, said my dad, or Miss Pommier in French, or Miss Sagarrondoa in Basque, which is, of course, not called Basque in Basque country but rather Euskara, a lovely and euphonious name for a language, don't you think?

Fifth grade: Sister Bridget Anne, who my mom estimated to be all of twenty years old, barely out of fifth grade herself, the poor child; why her superiors would assign her such headlong ragamuffins as ourselves in her first year of teaching is a mystery to me; you would think that they would let her bask in the adoration of first-graders for a while, to get her feet wet, before inflicting whole rooms of incipient thieves and mountebanks upon her. In general the nuns are the brightest light in the Church Eternal and not given to errors of judgment, unlike their compatriots in the male orders, who are generally and regrettably liable to arrogance and hubris, but in this case I believe the girl's superiors made a mistake, which by the sheer fact that it stands out so adamantly from the general run of their sensible operations is perhaps proof that they hardly ever mess up, bless their souls.

Sixth grade: Sister Everard, who had spectacles so thick and tinted that you could never figure out where she was looking, which was deeply unnerving, as now we boys were twelve years old and thought we were cool and dashing and a boy named Kevin casually lit a Marlboro on the basketball court at recess and was slouching against the stanchion trying to look like James Dean when a ball hit him right in the belly at high speed and he swallowed the cigarette and a few minutes later barfed so colorfully and thoroughly that he had to go to the nurse's office and then his mother came to get him and if you looked carefully you could see steam coming out of both of her ears and curling briefly over her head like the horns of a demon.

Seventh grade: Mister Kelly. First male teacher ever. Half the girls in class had crushes on him by the end of the first period (American history). The first teacher we ever had who could and did throw erasers at students, and he had a whiplike arm and amazing accuracy. He was over six feet tall, not particularly muscular but sinewy like Sandy Koufax, with a slightly sidearm motion and excellent command of his throws, so that he could wheel suddenly from the front of the room, with a deft twist of his hips, set his feet, and whip an eraser thirty feet to hit, say, Michael, smack in the chest, beneath his necktie knot but above the belt, and all this in an instant, so that just as your mind registered the fact that Michael had made a snotty remark to Mister Kelly, there was suddenly a puff of chalk dust around him, as if the very utterance of the supercilious remark had caused him to instantly smoke with remorse. This was the year that the Mets finally brought the young Nolan Ryan up to the big club, and the first time I saw him pitch I thought of Mister Kelly, for they both drove hard with the legs to generate speed, rather than depend wholly on arm-whip.

Eighth grade: Sister Anita, a slim intense woman with eyebrows like Frida Kahlo. When she was aggrieved or annoyed she would bring her eyebrows together like two vast armies meeting on a darkling plain and no matter what you were doing or thinking you would just sit there staring at the seething tumult of her eyebrows. She talked a lot about college preparation and which high schools we were choosing so as to prepare for which colleges and when Michael said that *he* was not going to go to college and that in fact in *his* opinion college was for geeks and loonies and that *he* was going to survive high school by the skin of his teeth, like his older brothers did, and then open a gas station or a gun shop, Sister Anita frowned in such a way that I suddenly understood the Battle of Thermopylae, during which thousands of Persians crashed into thousands of Greeks, obscuring the tiny path that had separated them; and then there was a great furor and uproar, and Michael was abashed, and the bell rang, and we all went home.

LIKE THE DEW
THAT BLESSES THE GRASS

The way when we are about to say the Our Father everyone hesitantly reaches for the hands of the people on either side, some of whom they do not know and would never hold hands with so boldly and nakedly in the world outside; and the way the people at the ends of the aisles step out into the aisle, with their hands extended, reaching for the hands of the people from the other side; and the way we all stand there, almost swaying a little but not quite; and the way we all elevate our handholding for the latter part of the prayer and then detach our hands, grinning a little at the fact that we were all just holding hands; and the way even the few men who are uncomfortable holding hands with people they do not know and would never hold hands with, hold hands with them; and so we are one in grace like the dew that blesses the grass, like rain on the parched and withered fields.

Or the way the daughter, age twelve or so, shyly reaches her arm out and slips it around the waist of her dad, who inches closer as he booms out the hymn in a voice like a tractor starting for the first time after a paralyzing winter, and they stand like that, with her arm around him like a vine around a tree, all the way to the end of the hymn; and for a moment I think I have ascended into heaven, and heaven is here, as Saint Catherine of Siena said, and who would argue with a woman who dug graves for the dead and nursed those ill with plague and walked with condemned prisoners all the way to the brooding gibbet? Not me, brothers and sisters; not me.

And the way we shuffle up to receive Eucharist and make faces at the moppet hanging over the shoulder of the mother in front of us, so that the moppet giggles, and this is a sound of pure ringing holiness, for where there is innocent laughter there is the Chief Musician, as He is called in the Psalms; and the way when we have arrived at the celebrant and he offers the host to the mother and grins at the moppet and reaches out his hand big as a gentle shovel to bless the child and she is not sore afraid but silent and smiling and aware that something sweet and cool is happening; then I feel the grace like dew-fall upon us, and upon the toy bear clutched in the child's arms, and the pianist who looks exactly like Agatha Christie, and the moth who is always circling the second light in the ceiling whether it is summer or fall or spring, but not winter; does he or she sleep away the winter, huddled in the sacristy, or cupped in the hand of the statue of the Mother outside?

Every single time I drink in the Mass I am given a new gift, if I have eyes with which to see: the sweet old shoes propped under pews when the kneelers clank down; the shaking hand finding a dollar bill for the basket, an enormous gift from one who has nearly naught; the man in the wheelchair in the corner who sings quietly with the most beautiful velvety baritone I have ever heard; the woman bent so far forward by illness that the priest crouches and bends to look her in the eye as he offers her the host, attentive and kindly soul that he is; the young woman who always comes alone, but in recent weeks wears an engagement ring; the father and son chosen to carry the gifts to the altar, as alike in visage as twins but one twice as tall as the other; the sheer spilling motley bumbled silly holy humanity of it all, ancient and ever new, theater and ritual, meal and story, some of the Words of the Lord written long before Jesus was born of the teenage girl Miryam, in Judea, in the time of Gaius Octavius, later Augustus Caesar.

Ancient and ever new, the same and different all over the world, spoken and sung every moment somewhere on this earth, in every language imaginable, with every music imaginable, and every sort and stripe of human being, and other beings too, like moths, gathered together to be washed by the Mass. Do we take it a little for granted? I do, we do, for it is as sturdy and available as a table, as regular as nightfall, as free as air; and every one of us has endured poor Masses, triumphant arrogant Masses, Masses that were mostly show and not so much humility and gratitude and food for the road, Masses that were merely tinny ritual, rushed through and rushed from; but this morning I do not take it for granted, for it is every day extraordinary. Did we see it with the eyes in our innermost hearts? For it is of us and for us, a grace like rain on the parched and withered grass.

MISSING MASS

In our family we went to Mass every blessed Sunday of the year, and here and there you would have to go to Mass during the week because of funerals or weddings or Days of Obligation or Masses to Open the School Year or Masses in Memory of the Faithful Departed, so that by the time I was fourteen years old and sitting in my bedroom late one night calculating that I had endured something like seven hundred Masses in my young life, I resolved to miss Mass the next day — to blow it off, to skip, to avoid, to evade, to dodge, to unattend.

This was so shocking a concept that I sat there for another hour startled that I was even contemplating such the idea. Was it a venial sin to even *think* about missing Mass? Had I effectively missed Mass by *deciding* to miss Mass, like you could receive the Eucharist by sincerely desiring to receive it, though you were not physically capable of doing so?

And then came the flood of much more serious concerns, like the cold fact that I was going to have to lie to my mom and dad about having attended Mass. This was inarguably a sin and, even worse, I would be *lying to my mom and dad,* who were people I much admired, despite my strenuous and aggrieved and often rude objections to their unreasonable demands for generally responsible and civil behavior; the nerve of them, to trammel my freedom so!

But the lure of missing Mass was not to be resisted, and I spent the next hour plotting the crime; I would simply prepare as usual, and behave in the usual surly manner, and insist shrilly on wearing the usual shabby clothing (the bellbottom jeans! the battered jacket with the buckskin fringe! the blue high-top basketball sneakers! oh dashing man of fashion!), and rush out of the house with four minutes to spare for a five-minute sprint to church, and then...then I would simply turn north, once through the small woods between our house and Mass, and head to the village bakery, perhaps, or just stroll unconcernedly along the railroad tracks, a free man, subject to no ancient religion and its pompous authority, bound by no rules and regulations, an independent spirit, a young man choosing his road for himself.

And this I did, my friends; this I did, sprinting out of the house in the direction of church, mostly thrilled at the success of my devious plans thus far, but with a tiny dark roil somewhere near my spleen or gall bladder; and headlong went I through the little alley behind the Murphys' house, and toward the small bedraggled woods behind the firehouse, not even a forest but more like an overgrown vacant lot; and right here, at the big copper beech tree that marked the entrance to the thicket, my plans went awry, for I discovered that the faint sound of sneakers I thought I had heard was my next-youngest brother Peter, who stood there panting, ready to resume our sprint through the woods to Mass.

If my first sin that day was the unspoken lie of my true intention, here now came my second, and far worse; for I took my brother north to the bakery, and not south to Mass, and I swore him to the active defense of falsehood if we were interrogated by the authorities; and the sweet rolls we ate were bitter in my mouth, for reasons I knew full well, down in my gall bladder or spleen.

Of course we were interrogated when we came home at exactly the time we should have come home; had we indeed been to Mass, for I was devious, and adhered exactly to pattern, so as to mimic an honest morning. Of course my mom and dad somehow knew I had skipped Mass, without any report being filed; of course they knew, somehow, and it tells you something of their grace and wisdom that they did not shout, or fulminate, or roar, or rain down coals of penalty. No: our mom looked me in the face and then went downstairs to do the laundry, and our dad gently asked about the readings at Mass today, what were they, Isaiah and Matthew, perhaps? And again I lied, for the third time that day I sinned, this time in word as well as deed; for I spoke warmly of the readings that day and even elaborated a little on their gnomic wisdom, and my father looked me full in the face and turned away from me; and I was filled with shame and sadness and went to my room, feeling some strange pain in my middle parts, down in my spleen or gall bladder.

A little later my dad came in and sat down on the edge of the bed and said quietly that we should have a conversation about Sunday Mass and probably I was now old enough to make my own decisions about attending Mass and that he and my mother did not think it right or fair to force that decision on us children and that we needed to find our own ways spiritually and that, while he and our mother very much hoped that we would walk in the many rewarding paths of the Church, the final decision would be ours alone, each obeying his own conscience; that was only right and fair, he said, and to decree attendance now would perhaps actually force us away from the very thing that he and my mother found to be the most nutritious spiritual food; so perhaps you and I and your mother can sit and discuss this later this afternoon, he said, and come to some amicable agreement.

I sat there next to him, amazed and then moved at his grace.

However, said my dad, you realize that it is wrong and offensive to lie to me and to your mother about what you said you did but did not do; and worst of all, you led your brother astray and made him lie also, and for that you ought to be thoroughly ashamed of yourself. You owe your brother an apology for that, and it had better be a sincere and heartfelt apology, too, if you have any ambitions to be a decent man in the years to come. Why don't you just sit here and think about the damage you just did to your brother's open honest soul, to his innocence, to his respect and love for you, and when you are ready to make amends to him, do so, and then we will all have lunch.

I sat there on the bed for a while, and then I did seek out my brother and apologize to him, and we all sat down quietly for lunch, and nothing else was ever said about this, until now, in this small essay; but the thought occurs to me that in a lot of ways I have been sitting on that bed ever since, pondering the way lies come so easily to our lips and spin so easily out of our ostensible control and stab the innocent and dilute respect and poison love and tear at that which so much wish to be, which is honest and gracious and reverent.

So rise with me now from the bed, brothers and sisters, and walk with me toward those to whom we should apologize; and then onward we go on the paths we each have chosen to the City of Light; and on your journey I wish you peace and joy unending.

X.

FIRST PRACTICE

You stood at the door of the gym with your mom, making sure that
this was the correct time and the place, and when you were sure you
turned and looked at your mom and she knew what you meant and
she gracefully withdrew, out of your eyesight; but of course she went
to another door and watched you through the window with her heart
brimming and tears in her eyes and she was proud and scared and sad
and proud; and some of the mothers went to the women's room or to
their cars to weep.

You knew one or two of the other kids also trying out for the
team, the first organized school team, fifth grade, the team you had
dreamed about for two years now, and you gravitated toward the kids
you knew but did not make a big deal out of it, because that would be
uncool and also technically you were in competition, so you said hey
and maybe touched fists but maybe not, maybe just a glance and hey
and then stood near each other, stretching, but not too near, which
would be uncool.

You knelt and tightened your laces for the sixth time this morning; and twice you wiped your hands on the bottom of your sneakers for traction; and the coach, who was of course someone's dad,
gave a short terse incomprehensible speech; and then Practice began
and you concentrated on making sharp cuts, and dribbling with your
head up like your older brother taught you, and taking only decent
shots and not wild silly careless shots, and boxing out in the lane and
setting picks and not only trying for rebounds but going up instantly
a second time for a rebound when the rebound was unsecured, like
your older brother taught you, because so many rebounds are available the second time; and never getting caught with the ball but making quick firm decisions to get rid of it or jump through a double-
team; and twice you made the right quick entry pass into the post
but both times the kid wasn't paying attention but you didn't say

anything or even grimace because you remembered what your older brother told you about prima donnas.

You did the very best you could not to compare yourself or measure yourself against the other players, or note who was good and who was hapless, or discern who else was playing your position, or glance at the coach to see what he thought when you made a good play or a poor play, or read anything into being placed on one team or another or being sent in or taken out, because you tried to remember your older brother's advice to Just *play,* man, play the way you know you can, a good coach will see what you are doing, you just play right, play generous, play with your eyes open for angles and space, and try to play *some* defense for a change, at least during the first practice, at least make a token *effort* at that end of the floor, and do not always be trying for steals, that is your biggest sin on defense other than not actually *playing* any defense, but that's something we can work on later, for now you just play as hard as you can and use your brains. Don't get rattled. Play quick but calm. You know what I mean.

I did know what he meant, and more than anything in the world I had wanted him to come to this first practice and just stand in the corner so I could draw some kind of sustenance from him but he said No, you have to make it or not on your own, man, you don't need me, I would just be a distraction, plus I am busy; and I was hurt, and said okay fine I will make it on my own, *fine,* but at the end of practice, when the coach quietly talked to ten of us one by one and I had made the team and I walked off the court tired and thrilled, there was my brother with our mom, and they were smiling, though you could see that she had been crying, just a little. She said she had *not* been crying, but you could tell.

OUR FEROCIOUS CREATIVITY

In the spring of 1943 my father joined a corporation with six million employees. He was paid fifty dollars a month for his work. When he finished his training, which included language courses at a college, he was suddenly promoted two levels and received a raise of thirty dollars a month. His employer also provided him with food (estimated at $1.50 worth a day), shelter (often a tent), equipment and clothing, full health care (estimated at $100 per month), life insurance, free cigarettes and laundry, free postage for letters anywhere in the world, and gratis barbershop privileges. Additionally his employer sent $28 a month to his wife, my mother, as a sort of payment for the rental of her husband; if they had had children then, which they did not although they would sure make up for it later, my father's employer would have sent forty dollars for the first child and ten dollars for every additional child, as a sort of payment for the rental of the father in the family.

In exchange for this fairly generous financial package, the corporation that employed my father for the next three years expected him to do his best in reading maps, interviewing former residents of places of particular interest to the employer as it sought to expand its base of service, reading reconnaissance photographs of such places, absorbing any and all information about those places (such as tide charts, topographic maps, road maps, geological surveys, and studies of regional flora and vegetation), and preparing plans for the corporation's expansion into that region, sometimes without the full cooperation of the residents; his last project for the corporation, in fact, assumed a ferocious opposition to this incursion, as the Army of the United States and its allies prepared to invade the islands of Japan and bring to a final and inarguable end the empire which at its zenith strove with tremendous force to control and enslave fully half the planet. We forget that the empire of the rising sun, in its fondest dream, saw itself as master of all of Asia, Australia, Oceania, and the entire Pacific rim, including, ideally, much of America and Canada.

My father would rejoin the corporation in 1951, after a five-year leave, during which he found employment as a journalist, and for this second stint with the corporation he was sent to Germany, where a second savage empire had been crushed by the Army of the United States and its many allies; an empire which, had it not been defeated, would have been slavemaster of all of Europe, Africa, Scandinavia, half of Russia, and, ideally, much of America and Canada.

In the end my father worked for the corporation for almost six years, during which time he was promoted several levels, finishing as a lieutenant, but you never saw a man who was more happy to retire from that corporation in 1953 and never again wear his uniform or crow about his accomplishments or bloviate about the way the corporation and its allies had inarguably saved billions of people from death and rape and torture and slavery. You never met a man more convinced that the violence at the root of the corporation was both necessary at that time and wholly a tragedy at any time, including now. You never met a braver man, willing, like almost every other man and woman who worked and works for the corporation to this day, to give parts of his body and mind, or all of the above, including his one lovely life, to help the corporation achieve its goals.

And you never met a man who, like so many soldiers and sailors and people of the air, are sure that violence is a terribly stupid way to solve conflicts.

Something to ponder as we honor the millions of men and women who served and serve with the American corporations that stand fast against bullies and slavemasters and murderous lunatics: those who fought and fight are generally the ones who are most articulate and intelligent about violence being the cruelest and stupidest solution to problems. Why is it that those who start wars were never in them, and those who were in them would never start another? Is there no lesson to be learned from what these brave souls tell us? Or will we forever send the fresh young brave to be maimed and die, when we could bend our ferocious creativity and imagination to inventing new ways to outwit the dim bloody brains of this weary world?

THE WORLD WILL SAY
YOU ARE SILLY!
BE PROUD OF THAT!

One of the great spiritual visionaries of our time was recently on the college campus where I work, and like everyone else on my campus I plotted greedily and deviously for three minutes alone with him, at least to chat grinningly and maybe even miraculously get down to brass tacks suddenly about how in heaven's name he and his friend Nelson Mandela managed to contain a savage civil war in which a million people might have been so easily massacred by citizens suddenly freed from a peculiar form of civil slavery after many years of being herded and beaten and cheated and raped and murdered by the grim slavemasters.

But, like everyone else on my campus, I did not get those three minutes because his campus handlers were officious humorless apparatchiks who had Archbishop Emeritus Desmond Tutu scheduled to the nanosecond (they had even calculated exactly how long it would take him to walk from building to building, defended from cheerful students along the way by a stern phalanx of these burly handlers), and it is to their professional credit that not once, for even a second, did the Archbishop get the chance to sidestep their meticulously laid plans.

But he did suddenly get down to brass tacks, near the end of a headlong and cheerful speech much interrupted by laughter; the former Archbishop of Cape Town in South Africa is a humorous soul, liable to laughter at the drop of a hat, and much amused by his own foibles and failures — a sign of personal and spiritual depth. Easy laughter at yourself and your own foolery, that kind of humility seems to me the final frontier, the open door to real wisdom, if we can shave our egos down enough to fit through the entrance.

He had finished his talk and the crowd was applauding vociferously and two or three students were shouting questions from the floor of the arena, in hopes that the Archbishop would entertain questions, though the somber handlers were shaking their heads no and moving purposefully toward the Archbishop to escort him off-stage, when suddenly he began talking again, in his high-pitched, amused tone; and the handlers stopped their approach, for you do not hustle Desmond Tutu off stage while he is talking, and the crowd quieted to catch these sudden clearly off-the-cuff remarks and the Archbishop said some things I do not think I will ever forget.

I have been a professional journalist for thirty years, and I am practiced at scribbling notes and carrying several pens and scrawling keeper lines that I know will sing later when I set them into the context in which they were spoken, but even I, a veteran journalist, an author and editor, sat there transfixed, writing not a single note, for it was instantly clear to me and everyone else in the arena that this man was speaking from the bottom of his heart, from the home of his soul, and to miss a word would have been a sort of sin and a shame — not because he was famous or even because he was wise, but because he was speaking so nakedly from the innermost chamber of his being.

For the first time in my journalistic career I feel abashed to paraphrase, but I must. So Archbishop Emeritus Desmond Tutu, when he spoke suddenly to the crowd at the University of Portland after his formal address, said something like this. We say all these things that we believe, but do we believe them really? Because they do not make any sense, of course. We say we believe in love, but so much in and around us is hate. We say we believe in humility and generosity, but so much in and around us is ego and greed. We say we believe in Christ, but we do not give everything away and follow Him through the narrow gate, do we? I am the worst of sinners in this regard. We say we live in His light, but so much is darkness. I am not delivering a sermon. I am just saying that we are so much in the dark. Many times I despair also. Every day there are times of darkness when everything

I say and think seems small and mean and only a swirl of wind in the dust. But somehow hope returns and we stand up and walk again. Perhaps that is grace. Our learned people write learned things about the nature of grace, but I think perhaps it washes over us all the time and we take it for granted. Hope does not make sense! But we continue to hope against all evidence! Could it be that to hope when hope is crazy is the purest grace? To believe against all sense and reason and logic, that is grace! The world will say you are silly! Be proud of that! Now I must go! I am always slightly late! God bless you! Pray for me, because I am a sinner!

And away he went, smiling, escorted by the prim handlers; but I was not the only man or woman or boy or girl who sat there moved and shivering inside, long after he had left the stage; and in a sense I think I may sit in that cavernous arena the rest of my life, pondering what he said.

THE MANNER OF HIS MURDER

My friend Tommy was roasted to death on September 11. He was a terrific basketball player and a wry wit and a gentle husband and the best dad ever, according to his daughters. Yet everyone who ever knew and liked or loved him is now sentenced to thinking about the manner of his murder. But this enrages and infuriates me, that his murderer gets to insist on anything when we think of Tommy, and I will be damned if I will put up with this any longer; so this morning I will edit the murderer out of Tommy's story, for the murderer was a foul misshapen spirit who bent his considerable brilliance not in service to creativity and community but to his monumental ego, the poor stupid slime, and Tommy was not like that at all, so we will stop thinking about the pompous ass who murdered Tommy and instead focus on my boy Tommy, who is alive and grinning right here on the page as long as I am writing this essay; and I would keep writing it for thirty more years if I could, and give Thomas Gerard Crotty the span of his natural life.

It would have been well-lived, Tommy's natural life. He was not the kind of guy who would stop too many nights at the pub, or hit on the secretaries, or play slippery games with the pension fund. He would have gained fifteen pounds because even though he tried to stay in shape and play golf and tennis and hike in the hills, he worked in finance, in excellent suits, and those guys just *do* gain the fifteen no matter what; not to mention that often the very best athletes also pack on the pounds when they get old, almost like their bodies are so relieved not to be lean humming extraordinary machines anymore that their bodies happily say *hey, sure, I'll have the onion rings on the side and another beer, life's short, man, and didn't God invent onions?*

Probably Tommy would have chipped in on a mountain cabin with his brothers, the rights divvied up so each family gets three weeks in summer and pretty much any other weekend they want. There would have been a discussion about renting a beach house instead, but Tommy played college ball upstate and came to love the wild forests along the Hudson and the velvety sprawl of the Adirondack mountains; who would have thought there was such shocking wild beauty so close to Manhattan, you know what I'm saying?

And Tommy would have gone to Father-Daughter dances with a smile on his face and tears in his eyes in the men's room that his girls were getting so willowy and beautiful and teenagery, and soon they would be writing college admission essays and one would be debating whether or not she should take the lacrosse scholarship from one school or the academic scholarship from another.

And Tommy would suddenly, for no reason whatsoever, slip into his wife's arms when she turned toward the stove in the morning, and as she laughed and protested he would glide with her in a sort of weird Tommy waltz through the kitchen and through the dining room and around the living room and even out onto the porch and the dog would get confused and excited and the girls would come running because their mom was giggling helplessly and their dad was grinning broadly.

And *that* is my friend, Tommy Crotty, you stupid arrogant bastard; *that* is my friend Tommy, as alive and funny and as happy as any man ever was in this world; and no one can kill his joy and grace and kindness and sly sidelong grin, *no one,* not as long as there are those of us who admired and loved him; and there are legions of us, more than you and your squirming ilk could ever count.

Let me put it to you this way, in this last sentence, in real clear terms, so even you will understand it, you who understood nothing of love: Tommy will always be alive because when we think of him we smile; but you will always be dead, because no one who thinks of you ever smiles; and someday, as the tides of peace and joy slowly rise to drown out thugs like you, no one will even remember your name.

XI.

A LIGHT IN THE DARKNESS

I was in a meeting the other day when a man across the table went into a high dudgeon about assisted suicide, which he opposed vociferously; he was still bitter and not a little enraged that citizens in our state were by law allowed to pursue such an ending to their lives, after slowly proceeding through various legal checkpoints.

He grew angrier and angrier, this man, and finally he was shouting about mortal sin and God's vengeance and cowardice and surrender and how suicide is just as much murder as homicide and about the terrible shame showered upon the poor survivors and the unimagined fires of hell; and I said nothing, and no one else in the meeting said anything either, and finally the man realized he was embarrassing himself and everyone else and he subsided.

I still wonder, a few days later, how much of what this man shouted was heartfelt and how much a sort of performance, which he rather enjoyed, I think; sometimes when people grow red in the face and begin to shout their convictions, I suspect they are preaching mostly to themselves and convincing themselves once again that they are incontrovertibly right.

And, too, a few days later, I still feel a bit of a coward myself, for I did not stand and coldly say then what I wished to say in riposte; but let me do so now.

What would you say, sir, if I told you that I understood the urge to extinguish the light? That I once lay in the dark, in terrible pain, week after week after week, with a broken back and the awful slowly dawning feeling that I would never be healed, never walk again, never make love, never lift a child, never spend another moment without savage stabbing pain so awful that in the worst throes of it I wept helplessly, unable even to pray desperately for relief? What would you say to that?

And what would you say if I told you that one afternoon,

propped in a chair by the window by my tender empathetic wife, I finally knew why some people commit suicide, and I understood those people, and thought perhaps I ought to be one of them? For if you too knew, or thought you knew, that you would never not be in pain; if you thought you would always be unable to rise to your best self; if you thought you would never be able to be happy and peaceful and easy and relaxed because you would never be out from under the dark; wouldn't you, even dimly, frightened and shamed by the very thought, contemplate a way out?

I did. I sat in the window and thought of being a cripple all my life, of never spending a moment without chains of pain, of always being a man who had to be carried and pushed by others, who needed to be cleaned and bathed by others, incapable of most of the acts by which we measure a man; and for a long time that afternoon I thought about taking my own life. I did. I thought about how, and who would miss me, and what I would leave behind; and I thought about sin, and cowardice, and quitting, about leaving the battle, about the terrible blow I would deliver unto my gentle bride, who would be haunted by my act the rest of her life. I thought about how I would never see my children and grandchildren. I thought about my parents, brothers, sister, nieces, nephews, troops of dear friends.

And yes, I thought about that which we call God, for lack of a sufficient word for such Boundless Mercy. I thought about the miracle of me, the gift of breath, the grace of imagination granted us, so that we invent ways to repair broken backs and illuminate despairing hearts.

Yes, I thought about God. I never did think of His vengeance or displeasure, His rage at my murder, the prospect of a billion years in the cold hell that is furthest from the burning of His love; but I thought of God, yes. Not of His anger, but of His love, thrown away by merely me; and I remember sitting in that window feeling selfish and ashamed that I was even pondering throwing away a gift beyond any measure, beyond even the idea of being measured.

I wish I could remember the one thing that made me finally laugh aloud and realize I could not and would not commit suicide, that I was just too ornery and hopeful and congenitally cheerful a man to quit, even when faced with what seemed like a life in the prison of pain; as I recall, it was the image, again and again, of my wife's haunted face, that I could not bear to contemplate; never was there a more gentle open kind soul, and she would be hammered terribly, and the very thought of her so hurt was unbearable. And that was that, as far as suicidal thoughts go; I suppose I am a very lucky man, for I only spent one afternoon in that dark room. I know, very well indeed, with great sadness and grief, how many thousands of people have been too often in the room, and are there right this instant, as you read these words.

So that is what I would have said to the enraged man in the meeting, who was shouting perhaps to be heard foremost by himself.

And I would add only this, then and now, to you: whatever you think of assisted suicide, whatever you think of the other poor despairing souls who hang and shoot and poison themselves, whatever you want to immediately say about sin or crime or selfishness, whatever you are absolutely sure that God thinks about this or other matters, remember this: Not one of us knows the prison in which they found themselves, the darkness from which they thought they could never be free. Pronounce sentence as you will, but remember that you too may find yourself in just such a prison, searching desperately for a window, a door, a crack of light, a hint of possibility that someday you will be released. Be tender, for love is greater than justice; and it may be that the quiet prayers we offer for these who are lost in this way are indeed the keys by which they are released in another world and brought home to That From Which All Light Derives.

REST IN PIECE

Since it's just you and me here on the page, and no one else can hear us, let's both cheerfully admit that we have, in moments of delicious melancholy, thought about our own funerals, and sincerely regretted that we will have to miss our own funerals, and wondered how many people would show up for our funerals, taking the morning off from work and wearing excellent black suits and dresses and maybe even veils and mantillas like in the old days. And let us also admit with a guilty smile that we have actually planned our funerals a little, at least secretly choosing some of the music that should be played, and we have also secretly thought about which six guys should carry the coffin, and which priest should be sentenced to being the celebrant, and whether to have the exit music be Booker T and the MGs or Joe Strummer, and whether or not to make one of the kids get up and speak for the family, and where your ashes should be scattered, and whether or not to have a headstone, and where that stone would be for the next century, and whether or not to leave money in your will for a proofreader, to be sure that for the next hundred years your meager remains do not reside under a stone that says REST IN PIECE.

Aw, go ahead and admit it — you too have lain awake sometimes, usually when you are in bed with a savage flu or down for three days with spinal agony, and you have grinned to envision most of the people you love in that lovely little wooden chapel, and all of your former basketball teammates sitting together in rough size order in the back, and your burly remaining brothers in the front, flanking your lovely bride, who is still making coffee for two in the morning and every time she does that she bursts into tears again; and even the dog is there, confused and excited, and wondering in his serene way if there will eventually be anything good to eat; and the priest, your dear friend and longtime pastor, is trying to stay somber enough to accomplish what in the end is a sacramental event with serious liturgical implications, but he cannot help but snicker as one friend after another gets up and tells a hilarious story about yet another unbelievably ridiculous nutty thing the deceased did once, oh my god remember that time we...?

And everyone is laughing so hard they are near tears or sliding just a bit into tears, that lovely shimmering place where you are laughing and crying at the same time — and isn't that what we both would like our funerals to be like? I mean, who wants sad? You and I both want people to start laughing and not stop laughing until the very end when finally our spouses and children lead the pallbearers out, and the pallbearers are grinning because one of them just whispered to the others that wouldn't the deceased be ragging us right now about wearing suits and ties, he would be all over our case, wouldn't he? And everyone starts to laugh again as the pallbearers cart the deceased out the door into the gentle rain, because the dog has leapt up and followed them, thinking that there might finally be something good to eat; and there *will* be something good to eat back at the house, and plenty of beer and coffee, and ham and turkey sandwiches, and those great snickerdoodle cookies, and terrific music all the rest of the day, as everyone stands around telling stories and laughing fit to bust. Isn't that what we both want for that day, people laughing? Because laughter is maybe the purest sweetest gentlest sincerest holiest prayer of all, isn't it? And if most of the people you love are laughing absolutely from their hearts all day long about the pleasure they gained in this life from your unruly existence, wouldn't that be the best funeral ever?

HIS SONG

The second son went off to college yesterday, in a flurry and hubbub of boxes and sneakers, and the dog and I are sitting in his room contemplating the remarkable fact that he is inarguably not here, after ten years of his being adamantly and sometimes snarlingly right here in this room, which still smells like sneakers and cologne and that weird orange pineapple basil mint guck he put in his hair for murky reasons.

The dog keeps poking his nose into the closet, on the off chance that the boy is suddenly there, even though he was clearly not there the last forty times the dog checked today. The dog is a student of miracles, and it would not surprise the dog at all if the boy suddenly stepped cheerfully out of the closet now; in fact, if that happened, you would see an absolutely delighted dog who would not spend a second wondering how this could possibly have happened, whereas I, a lesser being, would wonder just that the rest of my days and ponder how the second son managed to solve the atomization problem without any engineering knowledge whatsoever.

I pore over the wilderness of papers and books and posters and ticket-stubs and notes on his desk and on the floor and on the walls, and while part of me clearly remembers *someone* swearing and vowing that he *had* cleaned up his room before he went off to college the rest of me staggers when I find a small worn notebook filled with, amazingly, song lyrics. For a moment I think they are lyrics from the thumping sneering music he listens to all day and night; and then, with a stab and a startle in my heart that I cannot quite explain, I realize that they are *his* songs; that he has, for weeks and months and perhaps years, heard music in his head and tried his best to match emotions and stories to that music, and here in my hand is the astonishing result, a whole little worn gray book of songs by my second son.

Of course I am tempted to paw through the entire book; of course my first thought is that I will discover a great deal about my beloved son by studying his creative dream; of course I wonder if I will find references to drugs and sex, or dark wriggles of which I was not aware; of course some small part of me, the part that is a writer, is desperately curious to see if the boy has some zest and pop and verve and depth in his artistic effort; but then, somehow, in a rare moment of grace and maturity, I realize that I cannot paw through the book and I close it gently, with real affection and reverence, and put it back in the welter of stuff on his desk.

It's his life, not mine; and perhaps, much as we love each other, much as I wish to know every corner of every iota of his soul, there are some doors that should stay closed, unless and until he chooses to open them to me.

The dog checks the closet one more time, and then he slumps down by the boy's bed, as he has many times done before, and we just sprawl for a while, gazing at the posters, smelling the cedar wind trickling in the window, listening to the jays bickering in the yard, wondering why in heaven's name anyone would put that weird orange pineapple basil mint guck in his or her hair, and thinking about how many hours the boy in this room heard music in his head, late at night, when everyone else was asleep, and began to scribble words that would fit, would catch something of his own heart, would maybe be the first lines of the story of his long life; and then we hear the low murmur of our car, coming home from dropping the boy at college, and we jump up to go meet she who is the heart of the house. She will miss that boy the most, I think; he was, after all, once a seed inside her, before she sang him into being, into this bruised and blessed world.

MY FIRST MARRIAGE

My first marriage lasted almost an hour. It was a bright day in October. I was nine years old and my bride was also nine years old. I offered her a ring from a box of candied popcorn and she accepted with pleasure. We held hands. Her friends applauded. My friends were aghast. This was in the back of the classroom near where the coats hung. I remember the coats looming behind me, all different colors and shapes of coats, as if there were a gaggle of people standing there, watching the wedding. I remember the old wooden windows of the classroom and the fact that the windows were half-open and you could hear the faint shouts and burble of kids in the playground. It was lunchtime and the rest of the class, except the wedding party, had eaten hurriedly as usual and sprinted outside to play basketball and kickball and tag and stickball and a complicated headlong game called ringalevio that entailed chasing and grabbing kids and hauling them to a makeshift jail which in our case was a section of the fence that bordered the convent where the Dominican sisters lived when they were not edifying us.

I remember that my bride and I stood together uncertainly for a few moments after we were married while her friends made much of the moment and my friends made rude jokes as a way to express astonishment and fear at what had just happened. Then my friends led me away to play ringalevio and the bride's friends led her away perhaps to discuss trousseaus and cummerbunds.

I remember feeling a sort of relief, playing ringalevio, because I knew the rules of *that* game, and how to spring my teammates in the other team's jail, and how to twist suddenly like trout or a hawk when someone on the other team came pounding after me, and how to gauge a sprint through the other team's defense in such a way that I could feint one way and then cut sharply the other way at the last second, leaving the defender grasping at air as I tagged the outstretched hand of my jailed teammate and freed him from his unwelcome incarceration.

I remember playing the game so fervently that I returned to class with my shirttail out, and I remember Sister Rose Margaret tersely telling me to tuck it in as I stood in the front of the class with my new bride and Sister gave a short firm inarguable speech about how there would henceforth be no rings exchanged in her class, and no going steady, and no boyfriends and girlfriends, and no love notes, and no crushes, and certainly no talk of marriage, because those things were for later in life, after high school and perhaps even after college, and they would most certainly not be tolerated in her classroom, was that clear?

Yes, Sister, we all said, which were probably the two words we said most that year, and my former bride and I returned to our seats. I remember flushing, because I hardly ever flushed and when I flushed I felt like I was three inches tall with a face burning at one thousand degrees. I do not remember looking over at my former bride, but I do remember that at the end of school that day, after I had finished cleaning the blackboard and erasers as penalty for being married at lunchtime, that the ring I had given my former bride was back on the corner of my desk. I put it in my pocket and on my way home I threw it high into the canopy of a beech tree. Probably the ring tumbled down through the branches and was buried long ago, or maybe a kid or a chipmunk carried it off as a prize, but perhaps it caught just right on a thin new sprig, and the bud grew right through the plastic ring, and for a while a tree branch was wearing a ring and stretching out a hand, like a kid waiting to be freed from playground jail, but then one morning in late spring the ring cracked and shattered and fell off and everything spun on in its own way and its own pace, as it always has, and perhaps always will.

OF THE SKIN OF THE EARTH

We forget the sheer mindboggling sensuality of meeting the earth and its blankets of green and thorn and moist and flint, early in life; so come with me now for a moment this morning and cast your memory back to your first yard, the overgrown lot next door, the copse of woods across the street, the tangled alley, the dusty paddock, the dry wale, the thicketed banks of the unsung creek; no matter how urban our first childhood impressions, were we not startled and delighted and instant cousins with birds and insects, with mud and dust and soil, with the humble mat of grass, with the defiant ailanthus tree, with slugs and snails and ants and wasps, with rocky outcrop and permanent puddle, with the dense cling and yearn of the skin of the earth?

We crawled on it and then in it, and sometimes — frightened, awed, uncomfortable, prickled by the fear of forever — under it; we tasted it, and wore it as paint, and later bore it home on our clothes with pride, as evidence of effort; we dug and probed and poked and harrowed it and carved tiny towns and farms and rivers in it, back when we were the tiny emperors of tinier estates in sandboxes and beaches and the wild corners of yards where no trowel ever went; we jammed our fingers in it, and hauled up handfuls of it, and threw bits and shreds of it at each other and at animals and insects and brothers and walls and twice, unforgettably, unfortunately, at people's windows.

Loam and peat, muck and mire, clay and chalk, bog and sand, shale and stone: I sing the song of the skin of the earth. We staggered along barefoot on it when we first learned to walk, our toes and soles greeting it, being scarred and torn by it; we savored mud and moss, flinching from shards and stabs, learning a vocabulary of sensation that we still can speak all these years later; don't you sigh with pleasure when you walk barefoot on the beach, shuffle through lush grass, patter in water ankle-deep on the shore?

The skin of the earth is under water, the smooth rippled sand you can see in the sea, the gentle suck of the bottom of the pond, the pebbled splay of the bed of the creek; and the skin of the earth is right underneath the ground that lives in and on and over it; aren't you as startled and fascinated as me when you see huge scars in the earth from track-hoes and toppled trees? Do you slow down too, and gape into the mysterious deep skin of the sphere on which we whirl?

We take it for granted, this epic skin, this vast packaging, this unimaginable layer on lava; now that we are older, we sometimes look at it mostly for money, to see what we can take from it, how we can shape and channel and furrow and shave and sculpt it, how we can glean and harvest and mine what grows in and on and under it; but this morning, for a moment, drift back to when you were two and four and eight and twelve and ran and rolled and climbed and curled and swam over and slept on the skin of the earth, in all its astonishing forms and heaps; and ever it was patient with you and held you gently, as it has all your life with hardly a murmur, and will hold you still after you die, taking you under, or accepting your scatter of ash, to soak in and become new soil on which new children will run and roll and skip and sleep.

THE LONG OF OUR LEGS

Enjoyed one of the greatest of all human-being sights this afternoon — a child learning to walk, which is moving, poignant, comical, nerve-wracking (they *do* collapse head-over-teakettle or face-first sometimes, they do seem to have some sort of magnetic attraction to cement and concrete, substances on which no one at all should walk until you are well into your thirties). But mostly watching a child learn to walk is hilarious, although it also edged me toward incipient tears, remembering my own kids learning to walk, which was funny when they were staggering along the beach but terribly nerve-wracking when they were in the city, where falling down rarely goes unpunished.

I remember my daughter hanging on to my right pinkie so assiduously that even now I think that finger is a good inch longer than it was before I was a dad. Twin One shifting from stagger to sprint in about twenty minutes; that boy was in a hurry right from the start. (He actually slipped past his twin brother *in the womb* in the last few hours before they emerged, one minute apart.) Twin Two was apparently in no hurry at *all* to walk, and spent his first year in this world scuttling around on the floor, eating whatever came to hand, including a startling number of insects, and only starting to walk, I think, when his mother started to stagger while carrying his undeniable bulk. (This child is now well over six feet tall, but I think he weighs the same as he did when he was a year old; he's as tall and thin as a ship's mast, and there are days when I think if a brisk wind gets the drop on him it might bear him away to the Leeward Islands without undue strain.)

I stand quietly under a tree and watch the small girl I am observing waddle and yaw across the sea of the quadrangle grass; each step a new adventure and each, you can tell, still a newish idea for the legs and feet, which are still getting the hang of the thing; and the girl herself is entertainingly *not* in control of the engineering but seems to be riding along happily on top of her legs and feet, delighted to be moving upright. She sits down suddenly, with an almost audible plop; she leans a little too far to starboard, and capsizes briefly; her feet lose their way and she stumbles and goes down face-first in the grass; but she scrabbles up again diligently, weaving and waltzing a little, and meanders for another ten feet or so before gravity again hauls her down to examine the dense green mattress of the lawn.

Most of us staggered so when we were small, and we will shuffle and stagger again, eventually, if we live that long and are granted our last years hesitantly upright; and in between such pedestrian alpha and omega, we walk and run and sprint and hop and skip and canter and gallop, mostly with joy in our hearts and the wind in our ears; but this morning, for a moment, let us attend to the sheer sweet miracle of *being* upright, and moving along on our own power — an act we mostly take for granted. How lovely it is to be bipedalist and to stroll along, thinking of this and that, as the long of our legs carries us through the nutritious air. We were all this same muddy happy child before me in the grass, once, staggering up from the generous earth into the brilliant air, but after we became somewhat accomplished at it, we mostly stopped thinking what an extraordinary gift it is to be up and about.

But many people cannot do this at all; so many never even get the chance. So this morning let's say thanks and pray silently for those who cannot stride as we do; for at least for the few moments we carry them with us in our hearts here, they too are sailing along on their own feet, their legs scissoring rhythmically in a music as old as the first one of us who stood upright, long ago, and walked.

Our first steps were a momentous instant in the history of our genus, but I bet it didn't last long before down went that ancient child, head over teakettle, into the delicious grass.

THE CHAIRS IN THE CHAPEL

The news arrives that our little wooden chapel on campus will soon be fitted with pews, courtesy of a generous donor who does not like the sturdy old wooden chairs that have lived there for the thirty years since the chapel opened. Surely the pews will be lovely and new and redolent and perhaps even carved and planed and fitted with reverence; perhaps, as I would guess the donor had in mind, they will more accurately echo the churches of the past; and surely the battered old pine chairs have served the congregation well and deserve to be gently put out to pasture, to graze away the rest of their days in lazy sunshine, admiring the sparrows, who do not reap neither do they sow.

But this morning I will sing those burly old chairs, for I do not think anyone else will, and soon they will be bundled together on the back of a whopping truck and the last we will see of them will be their sad jounce and rattle and clatter as they are taken away to be sold, or burnt, or turned into avant-garde art exhibits about how we selfishly slay trees and force their remains to serve our indolent repose.

There were two hundred of these chairs; I counted them once, and well remember being startled by the number, for they were shy chairs, and did not take up much space, despite their adamant weight. They were ranked in rows of ten, ten rows deep, a hundred on either side of the aisle that they left open between themselves. They were ingeniously linked, so that you could, if you were young and strong and got a running head start, move a whole row at once, although that was rarely done for fear of scratching the burnished gleaming glowing wooden floor of the chapel.

Each chair had a thin cushioned seat — more of an intimation of a cushion than an actual serviceable cushion — and a small shelf beneath the seat to store hymnals and missals; although I have found cookies in that shelf, and reading-glasses, and once a bill for electricity, which was small enough that I paid it and thought myself a generous man.

If we guess that the chapel held some fifty people a day on average, a number that covers the days when there are five people for noon Mass as well as the funerals and vigils and concerts when there are far more people than chairs, then we approach half a million men and women and children who have sat in these chairs, and dozed and wept and agonized and prayed and spoke silently unto the Mercy in them, and suddenly we find ourselves seeing more than chairs. When we stare at these old pine chairs; we can see sacred spaces, refuges, docks where souls came to rest for a while during their long voyages; we can see small classrooms, perhaps, where children first became aware of the scent and shiver of religion and the song of spirituality beneath and beyond any words that we know. We can see tiny village greens where neighbors who arose from their chairs day after day at Mass shook hands and wished each other peace. We can see small wooden ships in which people of every age and stage have briefly traveled, sometimes bored, sometimes troubled, sometimes so moved that they could not rise and leave the chapel when everyone else did but sat there huddled in their coats even when the lights clicked off and there was no light in the chapel but that from the skylight and the banks of candles.

I am sure the new pews will be sturdy, and probably beautiful, in their way, and we will admire the way they give the chapel a new dimension, a new dynamic, new angles on the miraculous theater of the Mass; but I think I will always remember these old pine chairs, which served so many so well for so long and were themselves, in the end, holy things. Once they were the sinews of living beings in the forests here, and then they were carved into sculptures in which children of all ages could rest a while and contemplate a Love beyond measure or understanding. Thirty years they stood together in the chapel, day and night, washed by silence and smoke and music and voices, touched by maybe a million hands, and rarely did we spend an instant thinking of them; but we do now, in the last few days before they are trundled away, never to be seen again. Remember them with affection, and respect, and a quiet prayer of thanks.

XII.

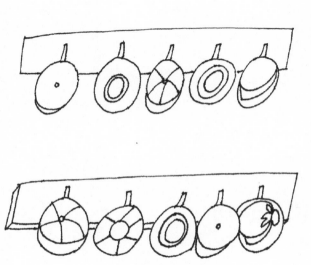

LIBRARIOUS

In the matter of early experience in libraries I suspect you are like me, and you remember pretty much every minute of that pleasure, from the first time you checked out books with your mother's library card, to the first time you used your own library card, to the first time you went to the library by yourself on your bicycle, to the first time you got totally absorbed by a book while purportedly looking for books to check out and curled up in a corner and plunged so deeply into the story in your hands that when the librarian came by, fifteen minutes before the library closed, and she said very gently *we are closing in fifteen minutes,* you looked up in some confusion as to what planet exactly you were on and who was this polite soul smiling at you and why was it dark outside when a moment ago it had been early in the afternoon?

If I was really memorious, in Jorge Luis Borges' great word, I would remember those first few books that swept me away, right out of my chair in the warm redolent corner of the children's section of the library long ago, in the back where the spruce and cedar trees looked in the window, but I do not remember the books as well as I remember the heft and splay of the books in my lap, their hard wings and their thin flittering insides, and the glory of their bright art, and the story so riveting that it made me forget that it was printed in words and built in sentences. I suppose my first few books were about animals, and basketball, and seas and ships, for those are things that absorbed me early and still do; but I do not remember the titles and authors and publishers. I do remember that I pulled them gently free from their upright fellows on the shelves and carried three and four of them at a time to my corner and arranged my jacket like a nest and huddled into the nest with a pleasure so delicious I can almost taste it now; I think I will never forget that feeling as long as I live.

Often I would read a bit of each of several books and thus arrive at the ones which would be pleased to come home with me, freed for a few days from their usual habitat; and then I would carefully restore the others to their homes in the shelves, being attentive to alphabetization and code numbers, for it would be disrespectful to the librarians to leave books scattered here and there, or stuff them willy-nilly into any slot in the stacks, *you would not do that at home, why would you do that in the library?* as my mother and father had so often said; and then I would carry the books I wanted to the counter, and proudly slip my library card from my wallet, flipping my wallet open and shut casually as I saw my father do, and be granted *one of the basic privileges of civil society,* as he said; and then I would gently carry the books home under my arm, or in my canvas newspaper bag, or tucked under my coat if snow or rain was upon us; and then at home I would carry them up to my half of the room I shared with my brother, and he would look up with a face of anticipation and pleasure that I would give a million dollars to be able to paint, and then, maybe in that lovely lost hour just before dinner, when there are no chores or homework and sport is done for the day, we would sit and read a book together, silently, sprawled together on the floor, trying to read at the same pace, so that one did not have to wait for the other but both reached to turn the page at the same instant — another delicious subtle pleasure I do not think I will forget as long as I live. In a moment our sister will come to the foot of the stairs and call us to dinner, and I will slip a scrap of paper into the book to mark the page, and I will be the one to close it gently, because *I* borrowed it from the library and it is *my* responsibility, but that moment is not yet come, though it is suddenly dark outside, and if you listen closely you can hear the table being set and chairs being drawn up and the clatter of pots and pans and our sister coming down the hall to the stairs; but let us end right here, before she calls us, because we are utterly absorbed in the story in the book, and being so deliciously absorbed in a story is a great and wonderful thing — as you know.

BEATLE BOOTS

When I was ten years old I discovered Beatle boots, at which point I suddenly wanted Beatle boots, because George Harrison wore Beatle boots (naturally enough, as he was a Beatle), and George was the coolest of the Beatles, not snide like John Lennon, or moonily romantic like Paul McCartney, or cheerfully silly like Ringo Starr. So I asked my dad for Beatle boots.

This was one of the great dad moments of all time, I feel, because my dad folded his newspaper and put it down and made a heroic effort to understand what I was talking about. We discussed the Beatles, and George's coolness, and the price of boots generally, and the nature of my days, during which sneakers and church shoes generally covered the bases pretty well, so that a pair of snappy black shiny sharp-toed leather boots, which were admittedly admirable pieces of footwear, said my dad, were probably not going to be of much use, unless my need was more of a social need than it was for actual useful footwear.

I confessed that this was the case, and we then discussed the relative merits of shoes, and how some shoes were actually not for utilitarian purposes at all but for show — statements, or subtle advertisements, as my dad said helpfully. Some shoes are ways for you to say something about yourself, or more accurately about what you wish other people would think about you, isn't that so? Many shoes for women, for example, are more psychological adventures than they are useful implements for locomotion, isn't that so? And certainly this is so for men as well — men who choose tasseled loafers, for example, are perhaps making a statement about class and status, or properly their *desire* for status, more than they are indulging a predilection for tassels. Similarly a man who chooses to wear the corporate norm in the way of shoes; is he choosing his footwear because he loves brown oxfords, or because that is what the other men wear and he wishes it to be known that he is a man like he perceives the other men to be and wishes to be perceived as such by them? And surely your own generation chooses its footwear as a way of communicating certain messages about the wearer — he who insists on sandals as a means of publicly claiming simplicity, he who insists on sneakers to indicate that he is not one to conform to perceived societal pressure, he who wears snappy black shiny sharp-toed leather Beatle boots not because they are comfortable, for they are not at all comfortable, or because he can afford them, for he cannot afford them, but because he wishes to announce to those around him that he is like someone else. Yet announcing that you are like someone else is awkward, isn't it? said my dad. You are not like someone else, and I would guess that the someone else you wish to announce you are like is not much or at all like whom you think him to be, either. Are you with me here?

I am not the brightest star in the galaxy, but even I, by the end of my dad's remarkable soliloquy, knew that the chances of me getting Beatle boots were nil and null. But that chat by the fireplace stays with me because I remember being so impressed with my dad's gentle intelligence and creative verbal chess that I did not storm and rage and whine and moan and whimper and stomp off to try wheedling Mom. I suppose I was disappointed that I would never have Beatle boots, yes, but I had to smile at the deft way in which my dad had said no without ever saying no. Even now, all these years later, I marvel that he was patient, that he was gentle, that he made a concerted effort to listen to and understand me, and that he then made me actually think about what I wanted or thought I did. How easy it would have been to simply say no; but it is the way he said yes to me and no to the boots that stays with me still.

There are many ways to be a good dad, but that way is at the top of the pile.

SKIFFLING

Saw a little kid with brilliant red boots skittering and scuffling and shuffling through maple leaves this morning, and I stood there, on our porch, above the street below where the kid was clearly not in any particular hurry to get to the bus stop, and I grinned as I watched him take every possible detour through the huddles and mounds and banks of leaves to get the best scuffling angle until he finally, with almost palpable reluctance, arrived at the end of the street, where there were hardly any hills and rills of leaves, and plodded down to the bus stop.

But he left his pleasure in scuffling and skittering behind him like the Cheshire cat left his smile in the air, and I stood on the porch, coffee pot in hand, remembering my own skiffling through oak leaves long ago, in concert with my two younger brothers, who were serious and tireless skifflers, especially my brother Tommy, whom we thought just might have a professional future as a skiffler if there was such a thing as a professional skiffle league; he was small but relentless, and when *he* went headlong into a substantive pile of leaves, for example the leaves that our neighbor across the street had raked carefully into prim geometric piles along the edge of his lawn, the leaves flew in wild amazing flurries, dervishings made even more amazing, as my brother Peter observed, because often you could not see Tommy in the middle of the pile, so it was if the hand of Our Blessed Lord Jesus was whirling through Mr. Townsend's leaves just for fun, although Mr. Townsend was not amused and stalked across the street to have a word with our dad, who silently made us rake the leaves back into piles again; but it was worth it.

It seems to me there were far more piles of leaves when I was a child, because back then you could burn your leaves and all the dads in our neighborhood would rake their leaves roughly at the same time, so there would be vast piles of leaves to skiffle through, for a while, until the piles were fired one by one, always on Saturday afternoons, it seems to me, so that the scent of burning leaves and old jackets and wet footballs and hot soup and new schoolbooks and homework done on crumpled loose-leaf paper with leaky pens all mixes together to spell Autumn in my memory; as does the sight and sound of a small boy happily scuffling through fallen leaves this morning, on his epic journey to school.

One of my own children was a terrific leaf-skiffler — this is the same boy who spent most of his time as a soccer player when very young, rolling in the grass because the grass was so lush and soft, the same boy who once said to me he was the best falling-downer on his team — but in his case I think he loved skiffling leaves not so much for the skiffle as for the fact that as long as you were scuffling through leaves you were not doing homework or laundry or dishes or anything else you were supposed to do.

There's a great wisdom here somewhere; so much pleasure is to be found in doing things that have no particular useful or utilitarian purpose but are done for the sheer animal pleasure of them, or simply because you can, or even *because* they do not have utilitarian purposes. Perhaps we are all always five or seven or nine years old inside and liable to staring at birds or clouds or suddenly skipping a little or gazing raptly at a river for no reason at all other than the meditation and music of its moving — or skiffling through maple leaves, just because they are there and our feet well remember what to do when confronted by such a tempting clump; and we do these things, smiling and feeling a little abashed, but not much.

THE MOST BEAUTIFUL BOAT
THERE EVER WAS

He is nine and I am ten. We are brothers. We share a room upstairs. Our beds are six feet apart. His bed is under the window because he likes to look at the shoulders and fingers of the burly maple trees outside. He will go on to spend his life working with trees and wood. My bed is in the corner because I like to curl up and read the Hardy Boys and Tom Swift and Jack London. I will go on to spend my life with stories and books. We spend a lot of time upstairs. Upstairs is for dreaming and downstairs is for everything else.

Today upstairs is the Pacific Ocean and we are building a boat using the slats of our beds, which we are not supposed to take out from under the mattresses, but we take them out from under the mattresses carefully, noting how they were laid under the mattresses so we can return them properly and not get that look from our dad. Our older brother says darkly that this look from him can stop time and quell hurricanes and frighten warlords in faraway jungles and this may be so. We use my mattress as the bed of the boat, and we erect masts made of slats, and we rig sails made of sheets and blankets, and somehow it all hangs together without collapsing, because my brother is already a wizard with things made of wood. Wood obeys his hands when he asks it gently to work with him. In later years he will ask wood to assume all sorts of forms and shapes, and each time wood assents with apparent pleasure, changing form with alacrity and grace. It's almost like the wood is delighted or thrilled to work with him and the wood strains a little to be the best wood ever when he asks it to be his partner.

In later years sometimes this will happen to me with words and sentences and paragraphs. I will learn not to command or dictate to the language but to ask it gently to assume shapes and forms that I dream about but cannot quite articulate, so I ask the language for help and sometimes the language is delighted at the chance and we sprint off together grinning and a little amazed at what was built on the page. This does not always happen, but it happens enough that you never stop hoping it will happen again. Often I think my books are like the chairs and tables and desks and beds and houses my brother has milled and planed and carved and joined and fitted and oiled and polished. In his case he gently asked trees to lend him their bones and sinews, and then he asked the wood to assume all sorts of lovely forms and shapes, and the wood did so, pleased to be working with such a patient wizard. In my case I went hat in hand to the house of language and asked if it could come and play, and many mornings out flew hundreds of words which spun and whirled and leapt and arranged themselves into laughing or snarling or dreaming parades and processions unlike they had ever done before for anyone else ever.

We take for granted that every piece is new in the world. Often I think that I am always ten and my brother nine and we are startled and awed and amazed at the boat we built. We still build boats, he and I, of wood and words; and if I know my brother, which I believe I do, he is exactly like me, and we stand in our workshops and stare at our work and think with amazement that this work was never done before in quite this way, and isn't that astonishing? Isn't that some sort of holy?

Soon we took down the sails and slipped the slats back under the mattresses and restored the beds to satisfactory condition so that our dad did not have to quell hurricanes and frighten warlords, but for a minute we stood together and admired the boat we built. Someone sensible would say it was just parts of a bed, but *we* knew it was the most beautiful graceful boat there ever was.

TWELVE HATS

Reached into an obscure dresser drawer the other day and pulled out, in order, the vaguely Maurice Sendakian wool cap my daughter wore when she was age two; the soft cotton watch cap she wore home from the hospital when she was age two days; the ball-cap one son wore from age five, when he became totally infatuated with the San Antonio Spurs, until age nine, when the hat had to be retired because it was falling apart and it nearly ended up in the rag bag but was rescued by the boy's father, who is a sentimental fool who cries when he opens a drawer and discovers what seems to be every hat that ever adorned the holy crania of his children.

Fourth from the drawer was the Saint Louis Cardinals ball cap our daughter unaccountably wore when she went trout-fishing so deep in the remote mountains of Idaho that you have to ride horses to achieve the Saint Joe River. Fifth was a battered green canvas ball-cap worn by another son, mostly at the beach, which is why this hat smells faintly of salt and kelp and ketchup. Sixth is a black Portland Trailblazer watch cap which both boys wanted to wear but neither wore more than once because it fit so tightly on your head that your face squeezed out pinkly below it like a sausage and when you took it off your hair assumed the shape of a castle in Spain complete with battlements and pennants. Seventh was a blue ball cap issued by the company, started by the children's grandfather, on the golden anniversary of said founding. Eighth was a ratty old green Notre Dame watch cap that had started life in the father's head (mine) as a student at that august university and then descended to each son on days of wintry emergency when they could not, by maternal law, leave the house without a hat and the only hat available was dad's ratty old college watch cap, which was down to a few threads held together by affection and nostalgia.

Ninth was a faded blue Geelong Cats watch cap which the

father (me) had brought home from Australia after falling headlong in love with Australian football, which, as he says many times a day, is the second-greatest sport ever invented by the devious minds of men, the first being, of course, basketball. This cap was also worn once by all three children, but no more than once, as it too, like the Trailblazers cap, had such a peculiar effect on your hair that after wearing it you had a powerful urge to just shave your head and start over from scratch.

By now I am both near tears and goggling with amazement that so many hats have taken up cramped residence in this remote drawer but, astonishingly, there are even *more* hats, poor things so folded and crumpled that it takes me a minute to identify them. The tenth hat is the blue soft cotton watch cap that the mother of all these children has been looking for on and off for a month, and how it got to be in the cellar of this drawer is a total mystery to me.

The eleventh hat is a red woolen beret that the mother of the children proudly presented to the father (me) of the children for romantic reasons, but the one time he wore it the children laughed so hard one of them had a coughing fit and there was a hubbub and a ruckus and the father (me) understandably never wore the hat again.

The twelfth hat is a thick red cotton watch-cap that the father (yes, me) wears when the temperature dips below zero, which it does in western Oregon every thousand years, so the cap has not, as yet, been worn, although you never know.

I stare at the twelve hats laid out on the bed, and my heart is tumultuous and time is all discombobulated, because if I touch one hat my daughter is two days old, and if I touch another she is eleven years old and unaccountably casting for trout, and here is my six-year-old son opening a hand-written letter from the San Antonio Spurs' gracious star David Robinson, and here are my lanky children rolling on the floor laughing at me in my red beret, and I am so thrilled and delighted to have all these years spread out before me but also so bereft and sad that those delicious exhausting moments and stories are now so firmly and inarguably in the past.

I slowly put the hats back into the drawer, folding each gently and respectfully and even reverently; for while they are only hats, made of cotton and wool and whatever eerie alien plastic the Saint Louis Cardinals use in their ball caps, they are of course not only hats — they are moments and stories of our children and so, eloquently, of love.

THE SPRINGFIELD GREYS

I was sitting with my mom yesterday at the old ash table at which she has been sipping tea for thirty years and she got to telling me a story. So come with me, brothers and sisters, as we walk with my mom, aged eleven, through the streets of the Borough of Queens, in the City of New York, on the way to see the Springfield Greys play baseball in the summer of 1933.

She is walking with her dad. He is a slight man with a slight mustache and a slight smile which he wears almost all the time. It is Thursday evening. The Greys play every Thursday evening at the Sherwood Oval, which sounds like an impressive park but only recently are there wooden benches for the fans to sit on. My mom says usually there were thirty or forty fans and a hat was passed to pay the players. Behind third base and along left field is a railroad embankment. People sit on the embankment to avoid having to drop nickels in the hat. When a train approaches, the announcer calls time and tells the fans on the embankment to get off, which they do, and the train rattles past, and the people scramble up again and the game resumes.

My grandfather buys frankfurters for himself and his oldest daughter. They love baseball. My aunt and my grandmother never go to see the Greys. My mother loves the time alone with her father. On Thursdays he comes home from work and the family eats dinner and then he and my mom walk from Laurelton, which once wild with laurel trees, to Springfield Gardens, which was once a vast sprawl of farms. They walk past shops and houses and gardens and the train station and churches and temples and stables. At the Oval they like to sit on the first-base side. You can see the players best when they sprint up the line toward first.

The Greys play the Bushwicks, from Brooklyn, and the Bay Parkways, from Brooklyn, and other teams from around the city; and occasionally they play teams from elsewhere barnstorming through

Queens, such as the Crawfords, from Pittsburgh, and the Homestead Grays, also from Pittsburgh, or the bearded House of David team, from Michigan. My mom remembers a pitcher who was terrific, and she remembers specific bunts and home runs, although not who hit them or what the score was or if they mattered particularly. What mattered was that she was sitting with her dad. He was smoking his Camel cigarettes and smiling, and they ate their frankfurters and talked about how bunts were gentle and home runs were violent. They talked about how a tiny bunt was better than a tremendous out.

You could tell that the end of the game was approaching because the light began to fail. Men put their jackets back on and children put on sweaters that their moms had made them carry just for this purpose. When the game ended, everyone applauded and the players waved as they ran off the field and my mom and her dad walked home to Laurelton through the gathering dark.

Mom finishes her story and sips her tea and says "I love baseball," and I know exactly what she means, which is not baseball as much as it is sitting with her dad and staring up at the little jaunty canoe of a mustache on his lip and worshipping him with all her heart and soul. They never ever left a game early, she says, even if the score was lopsided or the sky brooded with rain or it was awesomely hot.

Leave early, and miss a moment alone with her dad?

Never.

A BASKETBALL STORY

It's a little story, I suppose, and it happened a long time ago, but it keeps coming back to me, and every time it surfaces again from the pool of memory I find myself staring at it from a different angle. This fascinates me: could it be that all memories are alive and active and changeable, and they live vibrant mysterious lives in the depths of our flickering memory. Are they are like other people's children, who are new beings every time you see them again at wakes and weddings and parole hearings?

So then. We are on a basketball court in New York. It is summer. The court is near enough to the Atlantic Ocean that you can smell low tide, and gulls and herons drift over, and in the winter if you were to stop by the court to get in an hour of shooting you sometimes slide on a scatter of sand. It's just dusk; the light-towers are hissing awake. It's the first game of a summer league doubleheader. It's a good league; some of these guys will go on to play college ball. We have a decent team but not a fine one, because we are in the league for fun. We like to run and gun and try to dunk and we don't mind losing by ten. We dislike losing by more than ten, and if we fall behind by more than ten we go to our best player, who hauls us back into contention by himself. He is the most unprepossessing good player you ever saw. He has zits, and his hair is a mess, and he has geeky eyeglasses held onto his head with a black elastic band. He is a gawky guy without any discernible muscles, but he is a stunning leaper and a deft and efficient scorer when he wants to be. He rarely wants to be. He loves rebounding and that is mostly what he does, unless we call upon him to be a deft and efficient scorer for a while. He wears ragged low-cut black sneakers that he inherited from an older brother. He is the palest person we know, even after he spent the summer playing ball in the sun and going to the beach to ogle girls. He mostly wears a goofy smile and is an affable soul, except about his car. You do not mess with his car. We drive to games in his car. There is no eating or drinking in his car. There are no wet towels or wet shorts in his car. You do not take off your sweaty sneakers and socks in his car. These are the rules and, if you observe the rules, he is an affable guy.

Tonight we are playing a team we do not know. The ref tells us they are from the town where Julius Erving was born. Their center glowers at us when we come out for the opening tip. Our best player jumps center for us because he can jump to the moon. He wins the tip and we run our standard opening play which produces a baby hook for him which he never misses. My theory is that he never misses because he is shooting down rather than up like the rest of us. This time he rolls into the lane for his baby hook and just as he lets it go the other team's center smashes him in the face. It sure looks to me like a deliberate foul but the ref doesn't call it. (This is summer league and the ref may or may not be sober.)

Our man shakes off the foul and we drift back on defense. The other team works the ball to their center and he goes up for a hook also, and as he shoots with his right hand his left arm swings out and smashes our man in the face. It sure looks to me like a deliberate foul again, but again the ref doesn't call anything.

We walk the ball up, waiting for our man to adjust his eyeglasses, which have been knocked awry, and without anything being said we run the same play to get him the ball again so he can score on this horse's ass of an opposing center. But, amazingly, the same thing happens, our man hits his lovely baby hook and gets smashed right in the face so hard we can all hear the smack, and this time we bark at the ref, who snarls back and doesn't call anything, and we drift back on defense, annoyed.

But some little thing has changed, and this is the memory that comes back to me every few months or so. Sometimes I remember this moment and I see the light stanchions casting their huge webs of brilliant light on the empty softball fields adjacent to the basketball court. Sometimes I see all the guys who were on the court with me that evening. Sometimes I hear the last gulls and the first owls. Sometimes I smell the asphalt and salt and sweat and the marinating marsh beyond the floodlights. Sometimes I see the boy I was, shy and sinewy.

The other team went to their center again, and he rolled across the lane for a hook, and our man caught his shot and threw it right into the guy's face, as hard as he could. It was a clean block and the ref couldn't possibly call a foul, so he didn't, but the other team's center was furious, and he spent the rest of the game shoving and banging and elbowing our man. But I am here to tell you, without the slightest exaggeration or hyperbole or fiction, that the other team's center did not score the rest of the game. Every single time he shot the ball, it was blocked by our best player, who had a grim ferocious look we had never seen before, except in regards to his car.

Early in the fourth quarter the other team's center made a sudden smart play and stole a lazy pass from me to our point guard. This was at midcourt, where you do not expect a big guy to be lurking, nor do you expect him to be quick enough to steal a lazy pass, but steal it he did and, since we were up by about twenty points at the time, both of us guards just lazily let him go, thinking that the poor arrogant lump would finally get an easy basket and feel better about himself after being humiliated by the geekiest good player ever, plus it was summer league and who cares and there's no glaring coach pacing the sideline ready to lecture us about relentless perseverance and consistent effort and character-building and other such nonsense.

But as the other team's center cruised in for his easy basket, our best player shot past us and took off and pinned the guy's shot to the metal backboard so hard that the backboard shivered and there was a sort of dark baritone ringing sound.

I have no idea how many shots our man blocked that night, or how many points he scored, or even how many points *I* scored. I remember a lot of things about that evening, like the fizzling lights, and our man peering at his black elastic strap as he tried to get his eyeglasses back into place, and the way the rest of us glanced at each other as we realized we were seeing something we did not completely comprehend, but oddly it is the sound of that ball being slammed against the backboard that I think I remember best. It wasn't the sound of a bell or anything like that — the old backboard was steel with holes drilled in it, you know the kind I mean — but it was a remarkable sound. I don't think I ever heard that sound again, and even if I did hear the exact same sound now, it wouldn't mean what it meant the first time I heard it, on a basketball court in New York, in summer, long ago.

THE RIDICULOUS
REVOLUTIONARY THING

Heard a riveting speech at Mass this afternoon, and I was so moved while it was being spoken that I had the urge to take notes, but the urge to record ought to be subservient to being startled and moved, don't you think? The more we record our lives, the less we actually live them, could that be?

But sometimes we *should* share a riveting time with one another; so here is one.

It was the noon Mass, which begins at five minutes after noon because the priest who runs the chapel here is no fool. There were some twenty people in attendance, half of them college students, the chapel being smack in the center of a college campus.

It was a normal Mass and everything went along as usual until the sermon, at which point things became riveting. The priest didn't stay on the altar, as priests usually do, but came down the central aisle until he was smack in the center of the small congregation; and then he said, pretty much, this: Look, every day we say we believe that Jesus Christ was the Son of God. In one way or another we say this every day, at Mass, at blessings, at funerals, at weddings, at dedications, at prayer services. It's inherent when we pray the rosary. It's the foundation of our faith. We assume it in every act and gesture and word and deed of our faith. But that's what I want to talk about today. We *assume* it. Do we really *believe* it? It's awfully hard to believe, isn't it? It doesn't make sense. We have no real idea who or what or how God is, to begin with. And then we say that an obscure Jewish man, born in a dusty outpost of the Roman empire, was somehow also *the Imagination that breathed all of creation into being?*

How could that be? I don't understand and neither do you. It doesn't make any sense. Sometimes we should admit this forthrightly, and I think we should do it today. It's refreshing to remember that the idea that Jesus was the Son of God doesn't make sense and we cannot understand it. If we are a little more honest about it being incomprehensible, maybe we will not take it for granted. Maybe we should admit that everything we believe in doesn't make any sense by the laws and customs of this world. *Everything.* We believe that mercy is greater than justice. That doesn't make sense. We believe that death is not the end of us and that we will live on in some way we cannot understand. That doesn't make sense. We believe that love and grace are greater than violence and despair. That doesn't make sense. We believe that an obscure Jewish man died, his heart stopped, his body cooled, his blood congealed, his brain function faded and ceased, and then he returned to life and walked again among his friends. That doesn't make sense. That's not possible. You would have to be nuts to believe *that.*

But what if, today, we embrace the fact that all of this doesn't make sense? What if we stopped for a few minutes and enjoyed the sheer nonsensicality of it and remembered that it is a revolutionary thing to believe what we do; and what if we try to actually steer our lives by such not-sense? What if today, just for a while, we stepped outside our usual sensible reasonable logical selves and reveled in the ridiculousness of what we say we believe? Let's enjoy the silliness of it for a few moments! Let's laugh *aloud* at the illogical foundation of our faith and our lives! Let's *savor* it!

And then, just for a moment, all of us, together, today — let's really and truly believe it. Why not? Couldn't it be just possible that an obscure Jewish man was indeed part and parcel of the Imagination? Are we really so sure what's possible and what's not? I am not so sure, and I would guess you are not so sure either. Isn't that what life teaches us as we age, to not be cocky and confident and sure of what's possible and what's not? Don't we learn astonishing things about the universe and life and human beings every blessed day?

Well, then. For a moment, now, after I stop babbling, let's sit in silence and savor the ridiculous revolutionary thing we say we believe. Perhaps it's true *because* it doesn't make sense. Did you ever think of that? Perhaps if it made sense it wouldn't be revolutionary and it would only be a human thing and therefore small. But what we believe is so much bigger than mere human things that we cannot possibly grasp or comprehend it.

In the normal course of human life, the priest concluded, we cannot believe what we do not understand; but our whole faith and I hope, with all my heart, our whole lives, yours and mine, is based on *believing what we will never understand.* Today, for a few moments, in silence, let's savor and enjoy and celebrate and meditate on just that. It doesn't make sense! Isn't that great? Isn't that maybe the only road to salvation, to mercy and peace and joy triumphant, to evil fled wailing from this world, to love everywhere the victor, to God's dream for us accomplished?

Think about it. Think *hard*. Amen.

AVE MARIA

Stopped to see a sickly friend yesterday. He lives away out on the west side of the city. Yes, I grumbled at the long drive. Yes, I did. Shame on me. His wife was away for a week and there was a cheerful nurse there to keep an eye on things and make sure he ate something. He doesn't eat much anymore. He *says* he eats but he doesn't, really. He's half the size he used to be. He used to be tall and bony and sinewy and intimidating and now he isn't. He's gaunt and bent and scrawny and looks like a long tree branch with intense eyes. He's in bed all the time now. His hands are still huge, though. He was a star basketball player in high school. Long ago and far away, as he says.

My friend is pretty chipper today. For a while after the stroke he didn't say much, but today he talks about his daughters. Three living; one gone ahead. Even now, all these years later, it haunts him that his little girl withered and died and she's not in the photographs of the family since then. You can hear the hole in his heart when he says her name.

We only lost one game the year we won state, he says. To Cheyenne High. Boy, those Cheyenne fans. They roasted us from the minute our bus arrived to the minute we left. Boy.

My friend runs through some of the other guys on his team, who they are and what they are doing now, for the other two friends who are here with me; my eyes wander around the room. The photographs with only three daughters and not four. Not one, not two, but three rosaries on the bed table, all different colors. A shelf filled with the detritus of medical indignity. A photograph of the Casper High School State Champions 1949. Twelve boys, their faces narrow and their haircuts trying to be meticulous, but one boy's hair refuses to behave and another boy's hair you just know has been slicked down adamantly for the photograph and surely a minute later his hair leapt back up giggling and the other guys on the team lost it laughing and then practice started.

My friend is getting tired. You can tell. His hands are still gesticulating and his eyes are eager, but the rest of what's left of him is running out of gas. The nurse doesn't even have to come in and say something sideways that means we should go. He knows and we know we should go, but once we go he will be weary and half of what he used to be.

After we go, he will stare out the window into his garden, where there is a statue of the Madonna. She looks cold out there in the winter wind, but she is tough. She said yes when anyone sensible would have said no. She was the person my friend would talk to throughout his life when he was weary and broken, as for example after his little girl withered and died. I cannot imagine what the world would be like without my daughter in it, but my friend, sprawled here in front of me like a long skinny knobby bent burled gaunt tree branch, knows what that world is like.

We have to go. We stand up to indicate that we are moving toward going and he reaches out his huge gnarled hands and one of my friends, a tall lean priest, says *Let's go to Mary* and we hold hands, the four of us, and pray the Hail Mary. From where I am standing I can see the statue of the Madonna in the garden. She is wrapped in a cloak, probably because the wind is so sharp today. My friend prays with all his might. He is staring at the priest. You know how most of the time when we pray we are just chanting gently? He is not chanting gently. He is begging for something with all his might. He is begging for something we humans do not have words for. The way he prays is what the word fervent means.

We finish praying and there is an instant during which no one lets go of the other guys' hands. All the way home I think of this instant, and only late at night do I realize it is exactly like holding hands in the huddle before a basketball game. Just for an instant you all hold hands and say something and stare at each other fervently and then it's time to go.

A NOTE

Most of these essays and stories and anecdotes and musings and roarings appeared first in magazines, both paper and electric, in America, Australia, and Ireland, and with honest and heartfelt sincerity I thank the editors who allowed these pieces into the gleaming corrals of their periodicals. I am absolutely convinced that sharing stories is a *very* good road to outwitting violence and deflating arrogance and inspiring creative thinking and dreaming, and I don't think we as a species thank editors enough for their crucial role as story-shepherds.

So my particular thanks to Sudip Bose and Robert Wilson at *The American Scholar,* Sy Safransky and Andrew Snee at *The Sun,* Rusty Reno and David Mills at *First Things,* Father Gerry Moloney at *Reality* in Ireland, Tim Kroenert and Michael Mullins at *Eureka Street* in Australia, Richard Kauffman at *The Christian Century,* Cathy O'Connell-Cahill at *U.S. Catholic,* Kerry Weber and Father Frank Turnbull at *America,* Matthew Boudway at *Commonweal,* Kerry Temple at *Notre Dame,* Chuck Luce at the University of Puget Sound's *Arches,* Margaret Harmon at *Denison,* Christopher Cahill at *The Recorder,* Steven Saum at *Santa Clara,* Marc Covert and John Richen at *Smokebox,* Rose Berger at *Sojourners,* Mary Stommes at *Give Us This Day,* and Kristen Hewitt and Chip Blake at *Orion.* They were all wonderfully open and patient with my headlong prose, and for that I am very grateful indeed.

Also by Brian Doyle

FICTION
Martin Marten
The Plover
Mink River
Cat's Foot
Bin Laden's Bald Spot & Other Stories

NONFICTION
The Grail
The Wet Engine

POETRY
How the Light Gets In
A Shimmer of Something
Epiphanies & Elegies
Thirsty for the Joy: Australian & American Voices

BOOKS OF ESSAYS
Grace Notes
Thirsty for the Joy
Children & Other Wild Animals
Leaping
Spirited Men
Saints Passionate & Peculiar
Credo
Two Voices (with Jim Doyle)